Lost Souls: FOUND!™

Inspiring Stories About Pugs

Kyla Duffy and Lowrey Mumford

Published by Happy Tails Books™, LLC

Happy Tails Books™ uses the power of storytelling to effect positive changes in the lives of animals in need. The joy, hope, and (occasional) chaos these stories describe will make you laugh and cry as you em*bark* on a journey with their authors, who are guardians and/or fosters of adopted dogs. "Reading for Rescue" with Happy Tails Books not only brings further awareness to rescue efforts and breed characteristics, but each sale also results in a financial contribution to dog rescue groups.

D0448383

Lost Souls: Found!™ Inspiring Stories About Pugs by Kyla Duffy and Lowrey Mumford

Published by Happy Tails Books™, LLC   www.happytailsbooks.com

The publisher gratefully acknowledges the numerous pug rescue groups and their members, who generously granted permission to use their stories and photos.

The following brand names are registered trademarks and the property of their owners. The author and publishing company make no claims to the logos mentioned in this book including: Meetup, Frontline, Velcro, Petfinder.com, Skittles.

Photo Credits (All Rights Reserved by Photographers):

Front Cover: Phoebe, April Turner www.uturnstudios.com
Back Cover Top: Mark Nardecchia www.shagly.com
Back Cover L: Kingston, Mark Nardecchia
Back Cover Mid: Ping, Pam Marks www.pawprincestudios.com
Back Cover R: Ziggy, April Ziegler www.aprilziegler.com
Inside Title: Phillie, April Ziegler
P11: Phillie, April Ziegler

Publishers Cataloging In Publication

Lost Souls: Found!™ Inspiring Stories About Pugs/ [Compiled and edited by] Kyla Duffy and Lowrey Mumford.

p. ; cm.

ISBN: 978-0-9824895-9-8

1. Pugs. 2. Dog rescue. 3. Dogs – Anecdotes. 4. Animal welfare – United States. 5. Human-animal relationships – Anecdotes. I. Duffy, Kyla. II. Mumford, Lowrey. III. Title.

SF426.5   2010

636.76   2010903726

Happy Tails Books appreciates all of the contributors and rescue groups whose thought-provoking stories make this book come to life. We'd like to send a special thanks to:

Buffalo Pug and Small Breed Rescue
http://www.buffalopugs.org

Central Florida Pug Rescue
http://www.centralfloridapugrescue.org

Colorado Pug Rescue
http://www.copugrescue.org

Compassionate Pug Rescue
http://www.compassionatepugrescue.com

Green Mountain Pug Rescue
http://www.greenmtnpugrescue.com

Michigan Pug Rescue
http://www.michiganpugrescue.com

Minnesota Midwest Pug Rescue
http://www.mnmidwestpugrescue.com

Ohio Pug Rescue
http://www.ohiopugrescue.com

Pug Partners of Nebraska
http://www.pugpartners.com

Pug Rescue of New England
http://www.pugrescueofnewengland.org

Pug Rescue of NW Arkansas
http://pugrescuenwa.typepad.com/

Want more information about the dogs, authors, and rescues featured in this book? http://happytailsbooks.com

Table of Contents

Introduction: Gotta Have My Pops! 6

Older Than God, Spryer Than Ninja 13

The Mermaid 16

A Snoring Ovation 18

Old Man Krazy Legs 20

Foster Dogs' Best Friend 22

A "Snort" Break 25

Better With Baggage 26

Dump Dog of the Forest 30

Pickles on the Rocks 33

Fear No Moe 36

Tick Tock 38

Troll Doll 40

A "Snort" Break 43

Little Alien 44

Her Name Was Lola 47

Puppyhood Revisited 50

Mill Dogs 101 52

A "Snort" Break 56

Next Stop China 57

Remove *What?* 60

Pugmobile 64

George on My Mind 66

A "Snort" Break 68

She Was *My* Bug From the Start......................................69

Seeing Her Through 72

Ace of Hearts 75

A Rescue to the Rescue 79

Four to Adore 83

Doggie Soulmate....................................85

A "Snort" Break....................................88

Foster to Founder....................................89

Moe on the Go....................................91

A Bittersweet Tail....................................94

Fank, Who?....................................97

Sarge in Charge 101

A Gift from Lilo....................................105

A "Snort" Break....................................108

Scootin' Along....................................109

Patience Pays Off 111

Life Lessons 114

The Dog with Nine Lives 118

Chipper Brings Cheer....................................121

Pawdiatric Nurses....................................124

A "Snort" Break....................................126

Best Friends Forever 127

The Principles of Pug Ownership....................................131

A Reason to Hope....................................135

Puggy Problems....................................139

Puggy Problems....................................140

The Ugly Bugsy....................................141

Introduction: Gotta Have My Pops!

My life has always involved a dog, but I had never considered a pug. At one point we lost our basset hound, Misty, to cancer, and by the time I eventually came around to the idea of getting another dog, we had just seen the movie *Men In Black* starring "Frank" the pug. Of course, Frank's big personality and adorable head tilt caught our eye, and though I was considering a Pekingese, my husband said, "Why not a pug? They have short hair, won't shed, and are not such foo-foo dogs."

So Pugley joined our family at eight weeks old, and we quickly learned that pugs *do* shed. We also found that they quickly grab your heart and become an intricate part of daily life. Puppy Pugley fit in the palm of my husband's hand. As he sat in his recliner, Pugley slept on his chest; at night she slept in my arms. And even though Pugley had health issues—double hip dysplasia and a liver shunt—we were hooked! Lots of love, money, and several operations later, Pugley is greatly improved and generally healthy aside from some ongoing issues with her liver.

By the time we decided to take our first big vacation in many years, my love for Pugley had inspired me to become heavily involved in pug rescue. Within a year I went from being a volunteer for Pug Rescue of NW Arkansas to becoming the president. That wasn't where I had planned to be, but the pugs needed someone and apparently I was it.

Because of Pugley's health concerns, we decided to bring her with us on our vacation. I took a few extra days off beforehand to do some cleaning, which resulted in a trip to the shelter to drop off some extra sheets and blankets I had found in our home (our rescue's dogs are in foster homes and usually do not need these items). As my husband and I pulled into the parking lot, we noticed an elderly man on oxygen leaning on his walker. A fat pug was stretched out at his feet enjoying the warmth of the cement. The shelter wasn't open yet, and we speculated that perhaps the man was here to get his dog microchipped, which is a service the shelter provides. As waited in our truck, we watched the pair. It was clear they were best buds, but then I noticed that the man was wiping tears on his shirt sleeve. My husband and I looked at each other, and without a word we both got out of the truck.

We asked first if the elderly man was okay. He said, "Not really, but I don't want to take him in there. I'm afraid they will put him to sleep." My heart broke. I asked him what was going on. He said he lived in assisted living, and they told him if he did not pay a $200 pet deposit he would have to move. He was on a fixed income and could not pay that amount of money. I asked him how long we had to get it for him, but he said it didn't matter—he had to go to the hospital tomorrow for an operation, and he wasn't sure he would be coming out. He loved the old dog, but he knew he could not take care of him anymore.

We agreed that this advanced-age pug would be in danger of euthanization if the man left him at the shelter. All three of us stood on the sidewalk in front of the shelter and cried, while the happy fat pug lay on the cement wagging his tail. Knowing I had to do something even though we were leaving town, I thought of my employee who was house-sitting while we were gone and decided to ask her if she could watch him until I got back. She agreed.

So Pops came to our home and slept on my employee's feet while she worked on the computer at our house for a week. We planned to put him into foster care upon our return, but when we got back, Pops showed us why the man was crying—he was the sweetest, most loving, good-natured, quiet pug we had ever met. He had *Keratoconjunctivitis sicca*, or severe dry eye, causing him to be about 80% blind now, but that doesn't affect his ability to serve as an ambassador for pug rescue. His love of people and dogs alike shows just how wonderful a rescue dog can be.

Pops has even helped me place several dogs. People are always asking me if he's available for adoption, and my answer is always the same: "No, Pops picked us. He will be a part of our family for life. But I have another Pug you might be interested in…" And so the adoption process begins again and again.

As you can see, the love rescued dogs have to give is abundant. I hope that Pops' story and the other stories in this book encourage *you* to take part in the adoption process if you haven't already. Whether you adopt your next pug, make a donation to your favorite rescue group, or take time out of your day to volunteer, your efforts won't go unnoticed or unappreciated, especially not by our furry friends in need.

 *Reta Parton*

Inspiring Stories
About Pugs

Older Than God, Spryer Than Ninja

R oy, a fearless, independent pug, was one of the most amazing dogs of any breed I've ever met. I had filled out an adoption application specifying an older (10+) male. The rescue president called and said, "You wanted an older boy? I just got one in that I think would work. You wanna come over and meet him?" So Cj, my better half, and I drove over to the president's house. She always has a bunch of fosters and newly-arrived "hold" fosters (waiting to be picked up by their foster homes) around, so when a little, gray-faced, senior boy came up to greet us, we asked, "Is this one ours?"

"Nope," she said, pointing to the backyard, "See that little lump in the shade? That's yours. I'll get him."

She went into the yard, came back with an armful, and set him on the floor in front of us. Cj and I looked at him. We looked at each other. We looked at the president. We looked at him. Standing in front of us was possibly the most ancient creature on earth. This dog might have run with the dinosaurs. 95% blind, 100% deaf, gray all over, and roughly 120 years old, he looked a bit like someone had wadded him up and tossed him. (When we later took Roy to the vet for a check, his official, professional, highly-trained opinion of Roy's age was "somewhere between 17 years old and four years older than God.")

"His name is Roy. The adoption coordinator named him for her father because he grumbles like him. What do you think? You said you wanted a senior," said the president encouragingly.

"I think I want one that will survive the trip home," I replied, with a hint of doubt. "What's his story?"

He'd been dumped in a busy parking lot. Animal control had picked him up and called Ohio Pug Rescue, knowing he stood a less than zero chance of adoption at the shelter. The fact that he'd managed to not get run over was a miracle by itself. I really don't want to understand the kind of mind that could leave any dog, much less one in his condition. I can only hope that karma has something especially unpleasant in store for whoever left him there.

I looked at him again. He grinned at me, head tilted because he couldn't lift it up all the way. I sighed. Cj sighed. We melted, handed over the adoption fee, signed the paper, gingerly picked up the elderly beast, and headed for the car.

Once home, I rather expected a doorstop. At his age how active or interested could he be? But instead we got a dog that let nothing deter him. His attitude about everything was "*Me* do!" He didn't like to be carried—he'd walk, albeit slowly, thank you very much. Beds were no problem; he'd ninja-roll off them by walking toward the edge, reaching out with his paw to verify where it was, and then stepping off into space. He'd hit the floor fully tucked, roll to his feet, shake, and walk off. I never saw him miss a landing. He'd chase our toes and nibble on them if we were slow with his dinner, and Roy had an impressive grip! Cj would dance around hollering, "Roy, let go!" while I would giggle and remind her that he was deaf and couldn't hear her fussing.

He slept between us every night, and for the first two weeks, he'd wake me up with nightmares. He'd howl and shake until I'd pick him up, rock him, and soothe him back to sleep, reminding him he had been found and would never be lost again.

Adopting Roy turned out to be a great idea. He had a smile that could melt any heart, and he used it without shame. When I'd get home from work, he'd come toddling over as fast as he could, and he could get up some speed when he wanted! He'd get up close to see what shoes were coming and grin when he recognized mine. He had a loud, sharp bark that could shatter glass, but he only used it when his grumbling didn't get your attention. We got to love and spoil him for about nine months before he slipped off to the Bridge. He left about two years ago, and I miss him still.

 *Kyla Jones*

The Mermaid

My foster dog, Bubbles, came from an abusive situation that left her with untreated allergies, urinary problems, and a bad hip that needed surgery. Though she came through surgery with flying colors, recovery was still a long road. Luckily someone made a donation for water therapy on her behalf, which helped her immensely along the way.

Bubbles' swimming lessons were at a lake. She was afraid at first, but she quickly took to the water, swimming alongside ball-chasing big dogs. She became a great swimmer, and within a few months she was running and jumping without any hints of pain. Her rapid progress even amazed her vet.

Bubbles was vocal when she wanted food and treats. She was also an entertainer. I'd ask her, "Bubbles, where's your spot?" (Her "spot" was a laser pointer.) Boy, would she get excited. I've never seen a Pug move so fast! If it made noise or moved, Bubbles loved it, especially her stuffed, quacking duck.

Equally fun for Bubbles was the dog park. She had no fear and would happily explore on her own. Everyone she met fell in love with her "bubbly" personality, but for some reason an adoptive family continued to elude her. Sure, she had a few special needs, but couldn't people see that *she* was special? Weeks turned into months, and Bubbles continued to wait for her forever home.

One day, during a Pug Meetup at the dog park, a couple seemed to be watching her. They eventually approached me with questions about Bubbles and rescue, and after about 30 minutes, they asked to put in an application. I thought they meant that they wanted to volunteer with the rescue, but shortly after returning home, I received an application from them for Bubbles!

The family turned out to be the special one we had been waiting for. Bubbles' new home came complete with a pug sister and a pool! She would have lifetime therapy for her hip, and even better, her family continued to take Bubbles to Pug Meetups at the dog park and rescue events, so I still get to see my precious Bubbles from time to time. A previous foster dog's happiness is always the reward for fostering, and I'm lucky to see Bubbles regularly with my own two eyes.

 *Mary Carpenter*

A Snoring Ovation

Every summer our family goes tent camping for a week in our favorite state park. We, along with our dogs, enjoy all of the usual outdoor activities: hiking, biking, swimming, kayaking, lying in the hammock, and sitting around campfires. Ruby, our rescued Pug, is what we like to call a "lab at heart." She never wants to miss a moment and will do anything her big sister, Ella (an actual lab), can do. Well, being half Ella's size, it goes without saying that Ruby is pretty worn out by the end of her day. Most evenings she picks a cozy chair near the campfire and settles in for a snooze while the rest of us talk and roast marshmallows.

Within the state park, there is an amphitheater with live nightly performances of original musical comedies. Attending at least one show during our vacation week is another of our yearly traditions. Luckily, dogs are welcome at the shows since seating is outdoors. Ella finds a comfy spot at our feet and sprawls out in the woodchips to nap while Ruby takes full advantage of the opportunity to snuggle in our laps as we watch the show.

Not being much of a theater fanatic, Ruby typically sleeps her way through the performance. On one such occasion, people around us were thoroughly enjoying the show's quieter acts and were startled to hear someone snoring loudly. We'll never forget the surprise and delight on their faces when they looked around and discovered our adorable little pug as the culprit. I'm sure they were expecting it to be my husband!

 *Jill Geurts*

Old Man Krazy Legs

C ooter "Krazy Legs'" journey into my life started when he was tossed out of a moving car. Though they were unable to care for him, the kind couple in the car behind the one in question picked him up and took him to a shelter, hoping for the best. But Cooter's future looked bleak. Even though the shelter staff loved him, he was an older guy with one other major "flaw" that made him unattractive to most potential adopters: his back was crooked so he couldn't curl his tail, and though he could stand on his back legs, when he walked he bounced like he just run a marathon. He could move his back legs independently but he fell down—a lot. Nobody knew whether this problem was a congenital birth defect or a previous injury that hadn't been attended to before causing permanent damage.

I had started volunteering at the shelter a few months prior to Cooter's arrival and had already overcome the typical "I wish I could take them all home" syndrome that plagues most volunteers. Nevertheless, by chance, I was asked to go looking for somebody in a kennel I had not been in all day, and when I rounded the corner, there was Cooter, bouncing up and down on his front legs since he had such trouble with the back ones. At that moment I knew I had to give him a forever home. After some surgery and the removal of most of his lower teeth, he was able to come home to a big backyard and a doggie door.

Cooter is indeed an old man and he still has trouble with his legs. I don't know how long I'll have him in my life, but his hilarious antics give me something to look forward to each day, and I'll miss him when he's gone. Despite his "handicap," Cooter is a real go-getter. He has figured out how to dig under my fence and has gone on several adventures, which have luckily ended with a knock on my door by a neighbor who has rounded him up. He has settled into his new home with comfy beds to lie in, friendly laps to snuggle on, and healthy meals to eat.

Cooter has taught me that despite a dog's age and physical (in)ability, adopted dogs are loving, full of life, and always grateful because deep down they know when they've been saved.

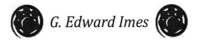 *G. Edward Imes*

Foster Dogs' Best Friend

A 20-pound, curly-tailed pug named Chico encourages me to help dozens of pugs find their forever homes.

Before Chico came into our lives, we were living with three dogs and three cats. Sadly, my son Jeff's dog, Peaches, fell ill and didn't recover, so a few months later, when Jeff was 14, he asked if he could get another pug. He was about to attend a new high school, and I agreed that a four-legged friend seemed like a good idea.

I started doing volunteer work with Michigan Pug Rescue (MPR) after my three children gave me my black pug, Yofi, as a Mother's Day gift the year before. Since we were looking for another dog, it seemed natural to contact Larry and Kathy Nathan, founders of MPR, to see if they had a match for Jeff.

"I have a lovely female pug named Jenny for you," Larry said, and after going through the adoption process, Jeff and I drove to the Nathans' house to meet Jenny. While Jeff hesitantly contemplated adopting her, I saw a beautiful, black-faced, fawn-colored pug sitting in a cage in the Nathans' indoor sun porch. It was Chico. He tilted his head, looked at me with curiosity and a smile, and almost appeared to be talking.

"What about this dog?" I asked Larry. He replied that Chico had just received a clean bill of health from the veterinarian and was now available for adoption. Chico's family had moved him here from Mexico to Michigan and for some reason relinquished him to MPR.

Larry took Chico out of the cage. This energetic, one-year-old pug ran directly to Jeff, kissed his face, and bonded with him immediately. Imagine my surprise when I brought two pugs home that day: Chico as part of our furry family and Jenny as our first foster dog.

Chico entered our home for the first time as though he had merely returned from a vacation. He gave every pet a lick, checked out the house, and settled in immediately. Before Chico and Jenny, our menagerie consisted of a pug, a poodle, and two rescued cats. Our new pets were welcomed additions. Though I could almost be called an empty-nester with two children already in college and Jeff not far behind, our house could hardly be considered empty.

Jenny was adopted quickly, and for more than eight years since the day we picked up our pair of pugs, we've continuously had fosters in our home. Retail stores have official greeters, and so do we—Chico! He may not wear a vest, but he knows what every new foster needs and offers it unconditionally. When they're scared, Chico hovers nearby. When they're restless, he comforts with play. He shows each foster where the water bowl is and waits his turn while they get their treats, knowing his new friends may need them more than he does. He shares his toys and occasionally even his favorite chewy bone.

Fostering these pugs is one of the most rewarding things I've ever done. People ask me, "How can you stand to give them up when they are adopted?" I tell them I give them up with pleasure. I love my foster pugs, but seeing the joy and expectation in adopters' faces makes me thankful for the opportunity to connect homeless pets with loving homes. Additionally, I know it will only take a day or two after a pug leaves for Larry to call me and say, "I have a pug for you to pick up," and then the cycle repeats anew.

People surrender the dogs who end up in my care for many different reasons: relocation to pet "unfriendly" housing, pet allergies, neglect of upfront research on the breed, new babies, impatience with potty-training, finances, etc., and though I provide them with love, routine, and safety, I owe much of our success in rehabilitating and rehoming these dogs to Chico's steadfast companionship.

As I'm writing this, Chico and my current foster, Handsome George, are lying side-by-side in a small dog bed. Chico has his head on George's back, and they both are snoring contently. It's a perfect picture of how Chico is truly the best friend a foster pug can have.

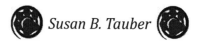

Susan B. Tauber

A "Snort" Break

Almost Human: The expression in Gunnar's adoption picture said, "Please take me home," so we did. This 38-pound pug needed to lose some weight, but other than that he was perfect. At night he listens to lullabies I sing to our two-year-old daughter, Maddison, and during the day he protects her on our walks and keeps watch over her at home. When the doorbell rings, he practically jumps out of his skin, crying and dancing in circles—it seems like he's about to start talking. *-Dana Palmieri*

The Birds and the Pugs: One day Zoey the pug picked up Tweety the parakeet in her mouth. My daughter and I screamed in horror, but the bird was completely unharmed when Zoey gently set her back down on the hardwood floor. On a separate occasion, the door to the cockatiel cage was not properly latched and our birds were loose for hours while we were at work and school. When we arrived home, we found both birds and pugs just hanging out with each other in the kitchen, as if it were the most natural thing for all four of them to do. *-Susette Cline*

Thinking Out of The Box: Lucy has a thing about the television. If she sees an animal, specifically horses, dogs, or cats on TV, she runs up to the TV, throws her front paws on the stand, and puts her face up to our 42-inch, high definition screen. She used to bark, but now she just whines, believing she has to get the animals out the box! *-Gina Gilliam*

Better With Baggage

My family always had dogs, so when I finally bought a condo, I was excited to get one of my own. As a conscientious dog-seeker, I researched many breeds before deciding a pug would be the perfect pup for me. Understanding that pugs are prone to numerous health problems, I wanted as much information about my new family member's genetic make-up and predisposition to common pug ailments as possible, which led me to purchase my puppy from a reputable breeder.

Unfortunately, even breeders can't guarantee the health of puppies, and the one for whom I'd waited so long had a terrible reaction to anesthesia and did not make it through his neuter surgery. Needless to say, I was devastated. I vowed I'd never own another pug, possibly not even another dog. I didn't think I could ever bear the pain of losing another animal again.

As time passed, I found myself yearning for the companionship of a furry body. I missed the feel of a wet tongue on my face and the sound of four little paws scampering across the room to greet me each time I walked through the door. I missed hearing the "ferocious" pug warning bark when someone knocked on the front door and the squeak, squeak, squeak of toys. I was finally ready for a new dog, and it absolutely had to be a pug.

This time, though, I had a new perspective on dog ownership. I realized that just as with people, there are no guarantees with pug health or lifespan, and for all the heartbreak I'd felt losing my puppy, somewhere out there was an equally heartbroken pug who had lost the comfort of his original home. I began exploring the Colorado Pug Rescue website, and some of the dog's overwhelming stories caused me to question whether I was truly ready to adopt. Could I handle a pug with medical or behavioral problems? Did I want a playful young dog or a lovable senior? Was I really prepared to help a displaced dog re-adjust to a new home? I had some doubts, but I filled out the application anyway.

I was soon contacted about Kobe, a 10-month-old, black pug who had already been in two homes before landing in rescue. I met Kobe the next day. He was in a foster home with three other pugs, and he was by far the quietest, looking like he'd rather hide than play. His foster mom told me not to be offended if he ran from me. After all, he'd already experienced abuse and neglect in his short life. Though he was a very sweet little dog, he had a hard time trusting strangers, especially men.

As I looked down into Kobe's sad, little eyes and contemplated his tragic history, I wondered if I could possibly provide enough love to make up for what he'd missed out on during his first year of life. Laying my fears to rest, Kobe answered my question for me by unexpectedly jumping right into my lap. While I sat with him in the living room of his foster home, I knew he would soon be sitting with me in my own living room.

I spent that night preparing my home to once again have a dog by purchasing new toys and lining a crate with blankets. The next day I adopted Kobe. I knew I had a long road ahead because Kobe was frightened and needed to build self-confidence, so I spent as much time with him as possible. Within a few weeks, Kobe was visibly more comfortable. He and I were already bonding, and though he was still hesitant with strangers, he began approaching other dogs on our daily walks. I decided to enroll him in a training class with the hopes of socializing him a little more.

Kobe loved his class and with each week became more outgoing. He grew into a well-mannered, lovable, goofy guy—everything I had hoped for. Yet I couldn't help but feel like something was missing. When Kobe began nipping at me and trying to play as though I were another pug, I realized he needed a buddy.

I went back to Colorado Pug Rescue and recently adopted Hercules. Not only does the pair endlessly entertain each other, but Hercules' presence has given Kobe the last bit of confidence he lacked. As I look at the two of them curled up next to me on the couch, our family feels complete, and I know that any future pet in my life will be from a rescue. For every home out there needing a furry critter, there is a furry critter needing a home just as much!

 *Sarah Keckler*

Dump Dog of the Forest

Buddy taught us that some of the best things in life are not only the ones we never saw coming, but also the ones we were absolutely certain we did not want to happen.

Dick and I had just lost our beloved rescue dog, and we were not "get another dog right away" people. We thought we needed time to mourn, but a foster mother for a local pug rescue, who was introduced to us by a mutual friend, had different plans for us. She called looking for a temporary home for Buddy, a pug-mix who had been found in desperate condition in a nearby state forest. He had *stage*

IV heartworm, a deadly condition transmitted by mosquitoes, and he weighed a mere 13 pounds, leading authorities to believe he had been out there fending for himself for about three months. Buddy's leather collar hung loose around his shoulders, and every rib and vertebrae showed through his thin coat. His eyes were dull and listless, yet his wonderful, long tail, which only curled a little (clearly the "mix" part), wagged at any gentle touch. There was no real reason that this "dump dog," the kind that has been turned loose in the woods by a heartless owner, should not have been put down except that his brilliant spirit kept shining through.

Buddy's foster mom spent weeks feeding him a special diet to rebuild his muscle mass and increase his chances of surviving the toxic injections necessary to treat heartworm. She joked that her own pugs were more than a little put out when they were served kibble while Buddy's special egg, cheese, chicken, and protein powder omelets were being made! When he hit 24 pounds, a much healthier weight, Buddy was ready to receive treatment, but he needed a low-activity household to survive it (the main reason dogs die during this treatment is from physical exertion that causes the fragmented dead worms to form life-threatening blood clots as they leave the heart through the bloodstream). We live out among beautiful cranberry bogs in a very quiet household, which is why she called us.

Our first reaction was to say no—it was just too soon. We had never had a pug before and didn't think we were "pug people." She called again, and again we said no, but a little more weakly this time. The next time she called we said maybe, and on the fourth call our answer became, "Bring him on over."

Fostering Buddy was not easy. His blood clotted, and he had seizures as the worms disintegrated into his system. We were sure we had lost him a couple of times. He needed a second round of shots, which few dogs can survive and some rescues will not pay for, but this was Buddy-the-Dump-Dog-of-the-Forest, and he wanted to live!

It took about six months, but when he finally became healthy enough to be neutered and adopted, we realized we couldn't stand the thought of losing him. This time, when the foster mother called to offer us the opportunity to adopt him, our first answer was a wholehearted, "*Yes!*" We even surprised ourselves with our change of heart, but Buddy wasn't surprised—he already knew he was home.

It's easy to see that Buddy healed us as we were healing him. I wish he could tell us how he ended up in the forest or how he was found with only days to live. He has a particularly gentle nature with the elderly, so we think that there must have been someone special to him in his past who was on in years. He's happy and funny and active, and he loves to run the bog roads with his new, little, pug sister, Tia. This once-emaciated dog is now more than a tad overweight, and his thick coat sheds everywhere. He can be pugnacious and overbearing, but his tail still never stops wagging.

Buddy's former foster mom is always amazed by his appearance when she sees him at the pug social gatherings she arranges. When he looks at us, his big, brown eyes seem to say, "Thank you," which is the same look we give him right back. I guess we are pug people after all.

 Marian Curtis, as told to Shar Clarke

Pickles on the Rocks

I wasn't looking for another pug. I already had a three-year-old pug named Mortimer, my first dog as an adult, purchased from a breeder. I don't know what influenced me to visit the Colorado Pug Rescue website, but one day I did, and I found a little sausage of a pug named Pickles. She was listed as six or seven years old, and her photo showed a round body with a tiny head on top. How could I resist a fat pug named Pickles?

I kept thinking about Pickles and asked everyone's opinion about whether I should apply for her. In the end I did, and we must have been meant for each other because the application before mine fell through, clearing the way for me to adopt her. Pickles and her foster parents were soon on my doorstep, and she was even better in person—adorable and rotund with plenty of attitude. I immediately fell in love, even though the first thing she did was pee on my floor! She is perfectly potty-trained, so I'd say she was staking her claim on her new home. The foster parents agreed with Pickles and said that she could stay. I was elated.

I don't know much about Pickles' background except that she was left in one of the overnight drops at the humane society as though she were a video being returned. My theory is that the family of an older person, who had passed away or could no longer care for her, had given her up. At 22 pounds, Pickles was in need of some serious weight loss. She was short and almost perfectly cylindrical, which wasn't a good shape for a pug. Her weight affected her breathing, and she could barely walk 10 feet without huffing and puffing. Otherwise she was healthy, so I began working with her by limiting her food and taking her on walks around the block and to the mailbox. Within about six months, Pickles had lost five pounds and looked like a completely different dog.

Now Pickles goes on longer walks, and she has no trouble breathing. The kids in the neighborhood know her by name, even though I don't know them, because she charmed them with her slow waddle and fearless attitude, which definitely deserves a mention. The human persona I've crafted for Pickles fits her perfectly and says it best. She is that older woman at the bar, the one who has been through the mill a bit, with hiked-up miniskirt, crooked eyebrows, smeared lipstick, and bourbon in one hand, cigarette in the other. She has that gravelly, three-pack-a-day voice and an attitude to match. It sounds silly, but when you meet her and see my friend's spot-on impression, it fits.

Pickles is always in charge of the situation, and every dog defers to her, even my parents' large Aussie. She knows what she wants, and she will look at you with disdain until she gets it. When she sits, she does so with her hind legs stuck straight out and spread wide, which is very un-ladylike and funny. She trundles over to strangers to sit on their feet and accept pets. She loves belly rubs and will fall over on the ground to demand them. I call this her "Tragic Pickle Death."

I don't know what Pickles' life consisted of before me, but I know that her life from here on out will be perfect and pampered, just like that woman at the bar's should have been. We'll never know if things could have turned out differently for her, but for Pickles, I know she'll never need a burbon to get through the day now that she lives with me.

 Jennifer Terry

Fear No Moe

In October of 2004, I lost both of my parents in a fire. Being the Indian rebel child that I was, I chose to cope by turning to alcohol and essentially had a nervous breakdown. Luckily, by the grace of God, I became sober about a year and a half after they passed away, and a year later I met my fiancé, Jason, who was accepting of the many things that I had on my plate. Because of my nutty family situation, Jason and I moved in together only a few months after we began dating, but we promised to support each other no matter what.

Jason helped me face my irrational fears, which were significantly hindering my life. For example, I was terrified of flying, so Jason took me on many flights. His "therapy" worked, and eventually I got over my fear of flying. The next thing we had to conquer was my fear of animals—particularly dogs.

We went to a dog adoption event shortly after I returned to college, and a pug named Moe stole my heart away. Of course, I was nervous about owning a dog, but as soon as Moe came home with us, he put my fears at ease. Our little pug inspires both Jason and me, teaching us lessons of life, love, and how special it is to be a pug parent. Jason is a surgical resident, and I am very busy with full-time school and a part-time job. Moe is always excited to see us when we come home from a long day, and he's always ready to take a family nap.

Moe was given up at eight months of age by his original owner because she did not want to walk him anymore, giving us a common bond of being displaced from our homes and families that makes us inseparable. While Jason works long hours, Moe and I are a like a team, conquering dinner and potty time together.

Moe has amazingly transformed my life and helped me conquer my fears. He drives me to do so many things that I've never done before, like attending puppy classes, going to the dog park, and helping out at pug adoption days. I'll be graduating this year with a degree in psychology, and I hope to work at a rehab facility, encouraging others into recovery. With how fearful I used to be, I never thought I'd be encouraging anyone to do anything, but now I know that anything is possible—especially when you have great companions to help see you through!

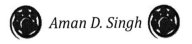 *Aman D. Singh*

Tick Tock

G reen Mountain Pug Rescue received a call about a pug whose owner was homeless. The person caring for Princess told me, "She has something messed up in her head. She spins all the time. And she has a frostbitten tail and nose!" I thought to myself, "Oh my," and I told my husband to go with me on this pick up because I didn't know what to expect. I could not *imagine* a pug with a frostbitten nose. I mean, come on, there is not much of a nose to begin with!

We drove the two hours to get the pug and could not help but laugh when we saw her. Frostbitten nose? Um, no. It was just a crusty senior's nose that had not been cared for, but the rest of the story *is* pathetic, as Princess had no hair on her tail, and the base of her tail looked like black elephant skin. Her backside was a bloody mess from her spinning in circles as she rubbed it on the carpet, and I immediately knew what her problem was. *Neglect!* Princess was infested with fleas, which I could see jumping all over her. We scooped her up, placed her in the crate, and began our long drive home, hoping all the while that she wouldn't pass her fleas on to us.

Princess was in so much pain that she just whined and cried for days. We gave her a flea bath, staying away from the inflamed areas on her backside, and rushed her into the vet the next morning for a shot to kill off all bugs and larvae. The vet gave her an e-collar, so she could not bite her tail and back end. She was put on a mild tranquilizer to calm her, but even in such pain, she would come and rub her head in our laps while we petted her and played with her on the floor.

Princess' ears were horribly infected, but more antibiotics and plain yogurt to help bolster the good bacteria in her system had her ears cleared up after a couple of weeks. With good food her hair eventually grew back, and her wounds healed.

Sometime during the process of rehabilitating her, we fell so hard for this 14-year-old little girl with so many health issues that we ended up adopting her. We know the clock is ticking against us, but we are enjoying every second of our lives with Princess and our other three pugs, two of which are also seniors. We live each day loving on our babies and taking pleasure in whatever time we are given with them.

 *Karen Powers*

Troll Doll

My "LadyBug" pug was a wonderful dog, so when it came time to get another dog, I was again on the lookout for a pug. One photo intrigued me: a skinny, wheat-colored pug-mix on a lead, leaning at a 45-degree angle, a crooked under-bite smile, and *huge* black eyes gazing directly into the camera. This "Chewy" was *not* the dog for me, yet her photo popped up every day, and I couldn't get her out of my mind.

One day I called the rescue that had posted Chewy's picture just to *ask* about her. I found out that Chewy had been rescued from a hoarder's home (the home of a person who collects animals compulsively) in Kentucky along with 70 other flea-infested dogs in poor health. After hearing the description of her former "home" and of her sweet temperament, I knew she actually *was* the dog for me! Too impatient to wait until Chewy would be brought to Chicago (only an hour away) in two weeks, I drove eight hours each way to Southern Illinois to pick up my precious little girl. She greeted me enthusiastically with love and kisses, ran straight to the car, and jumped in.

All skin 'n bones, she'd been shaved (those darn fleas!) and still had stitches from an operation to repair a hernia. This dog was part pug, part terrier, part Pekingese, and part *troll doll*! You see, when her coat started growing, the hair on top of her head stood straight up just like the trolls in my son's collection. When I joyfully called my best friend to say Operation Adoption was complete, Becky asked, "What does she look like?"

I had to be honest: "Like a pug who stuck her paw in a light socket."

By this time I had renamed her Luna, and when my other best friend, Joan, took one look at her, she laughed aloud and asked, "What *are* you?"

I did wonder why the rescue staff had christened her "Chewy" until her fur started getting longer. With long fur, Luna looked just like Chewbacca, the Wookiee of *Star Wars* fame. However, when her fur is medium length, Luna more closely resembles an Ewok. No matter the length of her coat, I think she is beautiful. At the annual Milwaukee PugFest, she is *fawned* over because of her, um, unusual good looks.

Two years later, this somewhat shy momma's girl sports a round little belly, regularly goes to Fancy Paws Spa, and "shares" her home with our other rescues: Zuma the pug, Riley the border collie, and Joyce and Percy the cats. She obsesses over tiny tennis balls, removes squeakers and fluffy stuffing from dog toys with surgical precision, and guards her home from all intruders. Luna loves roaming the dog park and playing with big dogs, particularly the giant Newfoundlands.

A true southern belle, Luna does not like the Wisconsin cold. When the thermometer dips below 40, the mere mention of walk sends her into her best defense mode: melting. This 17-pound pup suddenly collapses onto the ground like a sack o' spuds until I've wrestled her into her pink, corduroy jacket with white fur trim. Once properly dressed, she happily sashays around the neighborhood, leaving her special "Post-It Notes" in as many places as possible for other dogs to "read."

Nothing irks me more than when Luna chases the cats for no reason other than that she can. Nothing warms my heart more than to see her spoon Zuma or play bow to Riley. And nothing makes me laugh harder than watching Zuma and Luna race down the hallway, each with an opposite end of a tube-shaped toy in their mouths. "Chariot Girls!" we announce to the world. As Riley chases his tail and the cats hid under the dining room chairs, the girls end their game in a tangle of paws, wrinkles, flying fur, and overturned dog beds, and I know that everything is as it should be. My little Luna lights up my days as well as my nights. I cannot imagine life without her.

 *Dawn Balistreri*

A "Snort" Break

Puggie Pantry: One afternoon Buddy was nowhere to be found. I frantically searched everywhere—beds, closets, hampers, toy bins—to no avail and could not believe I would have to call the director of our pug rescue to tell her I had lost my blind little foster. After a moment crying on the couch, I walked into the kitchen to make my dreaded phone call. As I passed the pantry, I saw Buddy sitting on the first shelf among the paper towels and tissues. He was simply waiting for someone to help him down! I had never been so happy to see anyone before, and four years later I still keep in touch with Buddy's forever home just to make sure I always know where that puggie is! -*Lindsay Campbell*

Have Some Pugs Instead: I saw a cute, adoptable Lhasa Apso on the news, so I went to the humane society to inquire. They let me play with the dog but explained she had been promised to an elderly woman. Her daughter had yet to arrive to pick up the dog, but of course, just as I thought I might get to adopt her instead, the daughter walked in. A week later a shelter employee called and told my husband they had two pugs available for adoption, but they had to be adopted together. "What the heck is a pug?" was my first thought, as I pictured a bulldog with slobber dripping from its mouth. Of course, Rocky and Val, short for Valentine, turned out to be adorable, and we lived happily ever after together for five great years. -*Natalie Montoya*

Little Alien

After tragically losing our two dogs to cancer within four months of each other, our house seemed strangely empty. Though our Aussie, Darrin, had been elderly, Lilly, our English setter-mix, had been much too young to die. Through our sadness we told ourselves to enjoy the freedom of being dog-free for a while, but that didn't work. If a bit of food fell to the floor, it just sat there; there was no one to gobble it up, no one asking to go in and out the door, no one to sing silly nonsense songs to.

My partner, Dee, had wanted a lap dog for years. We'd never had a small dog of any sort, but after discussing a few breeds, we agreed on a pug. Michigan Pug Rescue's application was exhaustive, but we understood their cautious scrutiny of prospective adopters. While our application was being processed, we dropped by a "meet the pugs" event. Henry was two and hadn't yet been posted online, but there he was, lying upside-down and relaxed in the arms of the rescue coordinator, and they'd only known each other for a couple of days! Perfect, we thought, Dee's lap dog. I wanted him for Dee, and Dee wanted him because she thought I was smitten. We mentioned our interest to the rescue, not yet too attached, but soon thereafter we learned that Henry would be ours.

And so this bug-eyed, curly-tailed, little gentleman came home with us. For many weeks, I had to remind myself: This is a *dog*—I can treat it like a dog and train it like a dog—it is not a weird little alien. Henry's cuddliness and charm, his puggy seriousness, and his delight in our company worked his way into our hearts and onto our pillows. I had formerly been a "no dogs on the furniture" person, but first, I gave in on the couch. It was obvious Henry was used to being on furniture, and I got tired of arguing with him. Eventually the bed was not off limits either. When allowed, Henry likes to snuggle under the covers with his head on my hip. He was supposed to be Dee's dog, but he turned out to be mine.

It's some consolation to my partner that after we'd had Henry for a year or so, we adopted "my" dog. I'd wanted a collie for years, but Mary Abigail is now Dee's dog and as collies go, I will admit she's not exactly purebred. My "young collie" is more of a 10-year-old Boston terrier/pug mix. The only vaguely collie thing about her, and I'm really reaching here, is the way one ear bends over at the tip. Mary Abigail is funny, feisty, homely-cute, stubborn, bossy, and smelly—and we love her. Having lost our Setter-mix too early, it feels like a sort of balance to take Mary in and give her the old age that Lilly didn't have. Mary and Henry are great companions, whether they're wrestling, chasing, snoring, or waiting for each other to give up the best chew (one is always better than the other).

Our "1.5 pugs" fill our hearts and our home. We are thankful to their rescues for taking them in, for screening applicants, and for letting them come live with us. We're also grateful to our dogs' original families, who cared for them and then recognized that they couldn't anymore, making the difficult decision to let them go. Henry and Mary Abigail aren't perfect and neither are we. We celebrate them for that! We missed the joy and the work of their puppy days, but we hope to have many happy years together. Whatever fate brings, we're lucky to have them in our lives.

 *Julie Larson*

Her Name Was Lola

"Courtney, we have a dog for you to foster," said the voice on the other end of my phone as I drove home one early spring afternoon. My heart skipped a beat. I half listened to her as I pulled over to write down the information: five-year-old female, doesn't get along with small children, dog aggression but sweet personality, call the family. I called immediately and set up a meeting for me to pick her up the next day.

The following morning I couldn't talk about anything but my new foster—my first foster pug. I hardly worked and mainly watched the clock, which was moving unusually slow. I looked up directions to the house where I was to get her and checked the local news reports to make sure I wouldn't hit any traffic. Just in case my paperwork blew out the window or was the victim of a flash flood, I made extra copies and stored them in various places. I drove quickly and carefully as I made the 20 minute trip. When I saw the house and started to approach the door I suddenly became fearful. What if they didn't like me? What if their pug was awful?

The door opened, and I heard the familiar sounds of a pug guarding the house. There beyond the woman who had answered the door was a small fawn angel. Her name was Lola.

The rest of the meeting went quickly. I cried as the family told me about her. I could feel their loss, their hurt, and their grief letting go. I could tell they loved her so much that they wanted her to have an opportunity for a better life.

Lola and I drove to my house. She sat quietly in the passenger seat, and occasionally we would steal glances at each other. As I pulled in the driveway, Lola became excited. My pug, Molly, and Lola introduced themselves and quickly began a friendship. They ran throughout the house chasing each other; the "Pugtona" races I would experience every evening from then on had begun.

Lola was beautiful, and she knew it. If there was ever a diva pug, Lola was it. She walked around the house like it was her kingdom. My cats were her loyal subjects, and Molly was the little peasant girl who envied the princess.

Five months in, Lola was still aggressive with other dogs except mine. Additionally, she didn't like children except my nephew. We were resolved to adopt her as our own, and then the phone rang.

"I have a home for Lola," the rescue volunteer said. My heart stopped. I managed to say a few pleasantries as I wrote down the information, and I quickly called the family before I lost my nerve. We planned to meet the next day. As we drove to their house, I said they had to be perfect, or they can't have her. If Lola's not comfortable, we'll just leave.

We approached the house, and Lola seemed to know where we were going. She quickly ran to the couple sitting on the porch, and they cried because she reminded them of the first pug they had over 30 years ago. At that point I knew that Lola had found her home.

As the meeting progressed, I became absolutely sure that this couple was perfect for Lola, a realization that left my heart heavy. We planned the adoption for the next day, and as we drove off, I cried. I'd like to say they were tears of joy that Lola had found her forever home. I'd like to say they were tears of happiness that this family had finally found their new pug child. But I cried selfish tears of sadness and loss. My little princess would be leaving.

That night I watched her sleep, and I realized that I loved Lola, and Molly loved Lola, but there were other pugs for us to love, too. Somewhere on that cool fall night was an abandoned, cold, lonely, little pug who needed a home. She needed a sister pug who was kind and a human who was patient—she needed us. At that point I let Lola go.

Since then I have had many foster dogs. I still cry when they go, but it's never as hard as it was for my first foster, my first little girl who stole our hearts. Her name was Lola.

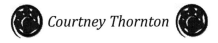 *Courtney Thornton*

Puppyhood Revisited

We had always loved pugs and for years had talked about making a pug the next dog in our household. So after we lost a dog to kidney failure, we decided to make good on our promise. We contacted Colorado Pug Rescue (CPR) and requested a pug between the ages of three and five, but they thought a puppy who had just been surrendered would be the perfect pug for us. She had been bought, along with her sister, from a pet store for two children. The children did not like the funny noises the pugs made, and so the family had crated them until CPR was able to take them in.

We met Lily about a week later. She was brought to our home, and we took her and our senior golden retriever, Red, to the park down the street to get acquainted. Red had never met such a small dog before, and at first he thought she was a brand new toy. He quickly learned that she was actually another dog, and this happy, sweet pup won all of our hearts. Back at the house, Lily took off like a bolt of lightning to explore. I had never seen a dog move as quickly as she did. Immediately Red took off after Lily and a game of chase was underway.

Red quickly taught Lily how to kill her toys and bark at those passing by on the sidewalk behind our house. They've been perfect playmates despite their difference in stature; in fact, I have never seen a pug who acts as large as Lily—it seems she believes she is a Saint Bernard!

Lily has reminded us all of what it is like to have a puppy around the house. She's always finding an exciting night light or tasty shoe to eat, having accidents in the house, and wondering what all the fuss is about when we find another blanket with holes chewed in it. Red is in awe of this little dog's energy, forgetting he was once just as energetic.

Lily has helped us move past the loss of one pet by filling our days with smiles and laughter, and she keeps Red young with constant games of chase. When Lily is not zooming around the house, she is burrowed under all of the blankets on our bed, sound asleep. The little girl for whom Lily was supposed to be a gift may not have liked pug snorts, but we know our home would not be complete without them.

Sharolyn Leeper

Mill Dogs 101

They came to me as PeeWee and Herman, fawn and black pugs about a year old. It didn't matter which one was which because these were not names lovingly chosen and bestowed. They were just something to call the puppy mill rejects who never sold and were instead given to the rescue organization where I volunteer.

I have three pugs of my own who help me socialize our distressed foster pugs, which is every dog who comes from a puppy mill. Mill dogs always need varying degrees of physical and psychological help before they can be sent off to new homes because their whole lives are spent in stacked 2' x 2' chicken wire cages where they receive no love, playtime, or adequate veterinary care. PeeWee and Herman were typical puppy mill dogs, but they presented an additional challenge in that they had lived their whole lives *together* in the same little cage, and families seeking to adopt bonded pairs are few and far between. My goal was to be able to separate them, allowing them to bond individually with their new families.

PeeWee and Herman could only be described as utterly terrified when we met. They huddled together in the back of their crate, trembling and whimpering. At home I put them in the yard for a little run, but they stood still, not understanding how to move freely—they had never experienced this luxury before. I spent about an hour outside with them, walking around, talking quietly, and sitting on the ground. They ignored every treat I offered them because they probably associated hands with pain, as the only hands that had touched them in the past were likely there just to grab them by the back of the neck and pull them out of their cage. Teaching them to approach a friendly hand would take time.

Their feet were flat, round, little saucers from standing in the chicken wire cages. They did not know how to go up the deck stairs, and once I put them on the deck, it took another ½ hour to get them to actually come into the house. I had been warned that they had yet to spend a night indoors, which was obvious from the look of fear on their faces. The first order of business inside was a meet-and-greet with my pugs, a good ice-breaker. I then fed them, took them outside again, and set up an open crate with a warm fleece bed inside. Giving them some calm and quiet, I checked on the pair later that night and found them huddled by the cold door instead of in their crate. Since they were still afraid of me, I decided to sleep in the kitchen with them for the next week or so to help them get accustomed to friendly humans.

Each day was more of the same as I slowly taught them appropriate indoor behavior, worked with them on potty training, and encouraged them to eat. They began playing in the yard, leashes became more familiar, and my pugs taught them a few tricks of their own (like begging for scraps). The stairs proved insurmountable until the second week when I found the pair suddenly on the deck with the rest of my pugs. Hurray! It was a major turning point, as if they were claiming the high ground over their past and were ready for a new future. From then on, their true pug nature started to shine through, and they turned into insatiable love-pugs, wanting to cuddle and be petted every second. Oh, and could they eat—another sign they were embracing their pugness! Finally, acting like the year-old puppies they were, they began to run and play with looks of joy on their smushed-in faces.

Because I had other dogs, this duo did not bond only to me. They greeted everyone who came to the house with curly tails wagging and snorts of genuine delight. Most astounding was that they no longer needed to be with only each other. I started taking one out for a walk and leaving the other at home, and there were no separation issues. I brought them for rides in the car, belted in the back, standing up to a window, tongue hanging out, faces feeling the breeze. These were not the same pugs I had brought home three weeks earlier

Confident they could be adopted out separately, I began looking for homes that complied with our rescue requirements. First, the dogs needed better names (I had never called them PeeWee and Herman). For advertising purposes I chose one of the great dog names for this region, Fenway, after our beloved park, for the fawn pug. The black pug became Gillette, after the stadium where the Patriots were dominating the league. I found terrific families for both dogs where they are loved and spoiled beyond redemption, and while I counsel people who adopt mill dogs that changing their names is okay because they're usually not attached to them anyway, these families decided to keep the names Fenway and Gillette.

I have never had fosters who had to go so far to become viable pets. Fenway and Gillette came to me as damaged animals, afraid of everything and everyone yet starved for human contact and affection, even though they had never known its touch. This is the nature of pugs. They were originally bred to sit on the laps of Chinese emperors, though these days they revel in sitting in the laps of average people who love them. Like all dogs they aim to please and make their humans happy, but for pugs that is their only job. They do not hunt, herd, swim well, or have any desire to run for miles. They love hearth, home, and family and a good treat every so often (or more often than not!). Fenway and Gillette could not have been further from that life when they arrived on my doorstep, yet in a month's time, they were sitting right there, having come up the stairs by themselves for the very first time.

I have fostered about 50 pugs in the past few years, and helping these two was the single most gratifying experience I have had. They touched me on a level I had not reached before with any pug, not even my own.

 *Shar Clarke*

A "Snort" Break

A Rainbow of... So that people (and apparently pugs) can "taste a rainbow of fruit flavors," Skittles heavily uses food dye, which we discovered after Zoey had found her way into a large Skittles bag. We have a sizable linoleum kitchen floor, but Zoey preferred to barf intensely bright food dye all over the light carpet and white fabric couch and loveseat. She was very sorry and promised never to do that again! *-Susette Cline*

Pug in Black: Riding home in the car, my new pug was so nervous that his curly tail hung straight down between his legs, his ears hung low, and he shook slightly. That all changed when a Johnny Cash song came on the radio. All of a sudden, his little tail curled, his shivering slowed, and he licked my hand. Well, he was a *black* pug, and apparently Johnny Cash was his favorite singer, so it only seemed fitting to name him after the "man in black." Johnny Cash, the "pug in black," quickly overcame his darkness to bring vibrant joy to our lives. *-Lauren Davis-Gorman*

A Bumper, Not a Chewer: The dog we adopted had been surrendered in a crate that he'd chewed through after interminable hours of solitary confinement and boredom. In our home he didn't chew and treated his toys very gently, grabbing one and bumping it into the legs of whoever entered the room to get the attention he so desperately craved. Earning the name "Bumper," our wonderful dog turned out to be a lover, not a chewer, and everyone loved him right back. *-Vonnie May*

Next Stop China

When my first pug, Mambo, died at the age of 14, I wanted to rescue an *exact* replica of my best friend: calm, friendly toward other dogs, easy to walk on a leash.

It did not take long before I was "just looking" at rescue websites. The pug I wanted was not available, but the rescue had an emergency situation and instead asked if I would foster that pug for the weekend. I agreed and met Fanny shortly thereafter. Fanny looked nothing like Mambo, and in fact, she couldn't have been more different. She was wild on the leash, did not favor other dogs at all, and the first time I took her for a walk, she tried to dig a hole to China while covering her pee. The grass flew everywhere! As the head of the rescue drove away leaving Fanny, her food, and her Pooh bear with me, I thought to myself, "At least this is only until Monday."

Unlike Mambo Fanny had no interest in staying contentedly in the roomy kitchen behind the baby gate; she immediately took a flying leap and busted the gate down. I purchased a reinforced gate, and we tried it again, but upon returning from a quick trip to the supermarket, the new gate was also on the floor, and Fanny was nowhere to be found. As I searched the house, I found Fanny standing on the back of the bed upstairs barking at a dog she saw outside. She had shredded a box of tissues, which now littered the area rug.

I was furious and determined to kick her out. I called the rescue and told them what had happened. They asked me politely to hold her one more day, as they thought they had a family that might take her. I reluctantly said okay since it was only for one more day. I went upstairs to clean the mess, and much to my surprise, I realized the mess wasn't actually tissues at all! Fanny had peed on the rug and again tried to dig to China. What I thought were tissues was actually white shreds of carpeting that had been dug up from the bottom of my purple rug! Now I was *really* ticked, though I must admit the ridiculousness of it all made me laugh.

As her imminent return to the rescue approached, Fanny started her "please don't give me back, I love you" routine by approaching me and putting her head on my shoulder. It worked, and when the rescue called to make plans to come get her, I shocked them by saying I'd keep her.

Since that day three years ago, our obedience lessons have paid off. Even though her temperament around other dogs is a work in progress, she is the love of my life. I am so glad it was not in God's plan to give me a carbon copy of my Mambo. I would not trade my *adventures* with Fanny for all the tea in China, regardless of how hard she has tried to get it for me.

 *Rose Van Der Velden*

Remove *What*?

My name is Norma, and I am a *Chug*: mostly pug and part Chihuahua. That's the new "designer" name for my breed, which really just means I'm a fabulous mutt.

As a particularly attractive Chug, my greedy humans decided I should have babies—lots and lots of babies. I lived in a little wire cage until it was time for the babies to be born, and then they put me into a warm place for a few weeks. That part was nice because we snuggled in a blanket, and I was given extra food to help me feed my family. But when I was just getting to know my little ones, those humans took them away and put me back into my cold, little cage, thus beginning the whole process anew. This went on for about five years until those crummy people finally decided I was not producing enough lucrative babies. They kicked me out since I was no longer of use to them, which turned out to be the best thing that ever happened to me. By then I wasn't so pretty: my teeth were rotting, and I had a dozen little, black nipples hanging down like dried up teardrops, but even so, a rescue took me in and placed me in a home with nice people and some great dogs while I waited for a permanent home.

The new place was great! After receiving some medical care, I slept inside on a bed and ran in a big yard. It took me a while to learn to play with the three other pugs at that home because I had never had a real friend before, but I eventually caught on. Shar, my foster mom, would cuddle me and tell me that she was trying to find the right family for me. I heard her tell people that I might be hard to place because I wasn't looking so good, but she knew I had a sweet soul behind my big brown eyes. After what I had been through, Shar wanted someone special who could love me and treat me right.

A family finally came to look at me, but they said they were horrified by my stomach and wondered if they could have my nipples *removed*. Seriously? When they called back to adopt me, Shar lied and told them that another family had taken me. She told me that they were not special enough for "Miss Norma," so I stayed with Shar for a while longer. Christmas came, and I was very excited to see a tree in the house—how convenient! I was later informed it was not meant for me, but why not?

About that time, a young woman named Rachel stopped by to see Shar's daughter, Jessi. They are best friends, and Rachel's mom, Beth, is Shar's best friend. Rachel and I just *fell in love*! I could not leave her side, and she could not stop holding me. Rachel had just bought a condo by the ocean, and she wanted me to hang out with her there. Imagine, someone *needed* me just to love them and be loved by them, without wanting to remove any of my anatomy! As a delivery nurse and lactation specialist, Rachel saw my nipples as beautiful badges of honor.

Rachel wanted to start the adoption process right away and bring me to my new home. But her mom told Shar that Rachel didn't need a dog in her life because she was getting settled in her job and new home. Shar felt Rachel's was the perfect new home for me, so she insisted that Beth meet me on Christmas Eve at the annual Open House where Rachel would also be. I was ready to destroy all resistance with an amazing display of cuteness!

That night when Rachel arrived, I flew into her arms, and she would not let me go. I wore a jingling Christmas collar, which rang as I licked her face. Then Beth and her husband, Mark, came in, fully prepared to stand firm, that is, until Rachel introduced us. I've never seen a human melt as fast as Beth did when we met. She gathered me up while Rachel told her my life story. As other people met me that night, most made jokes about my peculiar underside, and Beth rose to my defense like a woman possessed. She said that if Rachel did not adopt me, she would! What were once sad reminders of my old life were now symbols of dignity and courage.

A few days later, Rachel officially adopted me and brought to my new home a short distance away. Beth, now known as Nonni to me, was there to welcome me. I had a new bed just for me, pretty coats and collars, toys, and my own *Rachel*. I can sit in her lap and look into her eyes, and she knows that I love her as much as she loves me. When she has to work a long shift at the hospital, Nonni takes me to her house, so

I am not alone. If I accidentally gain a little weight, Nonni's Boot Camp marches it right off of me! When Rachel took an assignment across the country, she planned a route through pet-friendly hotels, and off we went on an adventure! My new life was nothing short of amazing.

Back home a young man recently came into Rachel's life. He had to get my approval first. While I don't necessarily want to share Rachel, more people loving me can't possibly be bad! Plus, he made clear that he fully understands my station in life when he bought me a life vest so I could accompany him and Rachel for rides in his boat. I still see Shar, and she likes to tell me how Nonni didn't want me but now loves me most!

I know that the people who adopt dogs like me say how much we have enriched their lives, and they could not imagine life without us. Rachel would say that too. But I need to tell her how much she changed mine. It wasn't so long ago that I was locked alone in an ice-cold cage. Clean water and enough food were luxuries I didn't often experience. My instincts and breeding tell me that I am a companion dog, someone who would love my human above all others by always providing her with friendship and comfort. I truly don't need designer coats, boundless food, toys, and an HDTV tuned to Animal Planet to answer this calling (but I'll take it!). I am happiest and most complete when I am sleeping beside Rachel on the couch, with both of us heaving a deep sigh of satisfaction and peace.

My teardrops, those badges of honor, are fortunately still with me, but thanks to Rachel, any tears I may have cried in the past have long since been wiped away.

 Norma,
translated by beloved foster mom,
Shar Clarke

Pugmobile

Jump in the car with my three "used" pugs and me, and you'll see they're as different as different can be. We're on our way to the groomer.

In the backseat you'll find Miss Maribel, a petrified, retired puppy mill breeder. She sits as still as a statue with no movement whatsoever. Wait, yes, she is breathing. Good!

Next is Boomie, an owner surrender and couch potato, who becomes a canine ping pong ball in the car. He *hates* car rides and is currently bouncing to and fro while emitting a soft, pathetic whine. He loves to bark, but Mommy does not allow that! In his bouncing frenzy he has a total disregard for the comfort of his fellow pug passengers.

Finally take a good look at Beau, who was surrendered by his owners at 13 years young. He's now almost 15, and the resident deputy dog. He's sitting by the window as happy as can be, and despite being deaf and blind, he's "watching" the world go by and wagging his big, floppy tail. One can almost hear him singing our car ride song: "Going for a ride. Going for a ride. Me and the posse are going for a ride!"

We make it to the groomer, but do you dare join us for the return trip home? Come on, chicken!

 *Beth Herrick*

George on My Mind

When you enter my house, you are inevitably greeted by a bunch of boys: Chase, Christian, Paxton, Brody (humans), and George (canine). While sometimes you may encounter a somewhat grumpy toddler, you are always sure to get a happy and excited greeting from our six-year-old pug, George.

We began thinking about getting a dog after my cousin was killed in her home by a drugged-up man. Her untimely death had a significant impact on me, and I wasn't feeling as safe at home as I used to. We contemplated getting a security system, but those didn't have great response times and were rather expensive. We opted instead to look into getting a dog and hoped we could find one as wonderful as our last pug, Bosley.

After searching the net, I found a pug who looked amazingly like our old pup. I sent an inquiry to the rescue listing him and a few weeks later heard back that he was available. We met him shortly thereafter, and he seemed to be a perfect match.

George had been with two families before coming to his forever home with us. The other families surrendered him for marking inside their homes and stated that a home with kids wouldn't be good for him. It turned out that those families, with schedules that didn't allow them to provide George with the attention he needed in order to feel secure, were just not the right fit. After a few months in our home, George's sweet, playful personality emerged. As his confidence grew, he stopped "saving" his food in case there wouldn't be more and became a better eater. We diligently reminded him that marking indoors was not appropriate, and now it's been over a year since he has marked in our home.

George proved to be absolutely wonderful with children. When my youngest was a mere three weeks old, he and George would happily nap together on the couch. Additionally he was infinitely patient when my oldest was around three and learning how to behave with a doggy in the house. George spends the day snuggling with whoever is nearby and keeps us safe with his protective bark at night. He recently went on a trip with us to Estes Park, and I think his favorite part was the car ride. He loves to climb up in the back window and sunbathe while we head toward our destination.

If I'm having a hard day, I know I can count on George for an understanding look and a comforting snuggle. He is a friend for me, an alarm clock for the boys, a garbage disposal for the leftover chicken, and a protector for my family. He had a long search to finally make it to us, but we think it was worth the wait and believe that if he could talk, he'd agree.

 *Claire Clark-Cox*

A "Snort" Break

Itchy and Snatchy: "Scratch. Right there. No! A little towards my tail. Other side. Other side! Yes! Yes! Right there!" Every day, a million times a day, that's our routine. Mr. Baxter Wilson doesn't want treats, and he doesn't want to sit on my lap. He wants to be scratched. First, his left side. Then, his right side. Wait five minutes. Repeat. Mr. Wilson hates the outdoors, and if left to his own devices, he'll steal all the pillows in the house to make a bed. He takes them off the beds and couches, piling them as high as he can in a corner of the living room. Then, before we realize what's happening, he's fast asleep. Not only has he stolen all my pillows, he has also stolen my heart. -*Victoria Lundgren*

Pug Poetry: My adopted Pug, Reggie, "dictated" this short poem to me between happy, grunty, munching noises at dinnertime:

All for me,
Beautiful big dish.
My love,
Food!

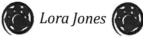 *Lora Jones*

She Was *My* Bug From the Start

It was a cool, wet day when I was called out on another run to pick up a dog. I was working for Greenfield/Hancock Animal Control as a control officer, and as usual, I hadn't been told anything about this dog. I assumed it would be large since most strays are, but when I arrived at the address I was given and looked around, I didn't see any dogs. It wasn't until I got out of my truck and heard a little, angry bark, that I was convinced a dog was even nearby. I followed the noise and came upon a small, muddy, sopping wet dog, tied with a large, heavy rope to the door handle of a car.

I untied her and looped a small slip lead around the fawn-colored dog's neck. She looked at me sadly with big eyes and licked my face as I dried her with a towel. Like I had so many times before, I lost my heart to this dog, and of course, she rode on the front seat with me instead of in one of the kennel compartments in the back. Upon returning to the department, she hung out in my office as she was booked into the kennel.

This little girl looked so much like my first dog, which I had bought years ago on my 8th birthday from a small kennel in my Florida town. When we moved back to Indiana, we brought her with us, but she was stolen out of my aunt's backyard. We looked high and low and advertised her everywhere, but we were never able to get her back. So needless to say, it did not take long for this new dog to wiggle her way into my heart.

The weekend came, and no one had claimed her, so I took her home with me. In addition to my animal control job, I have my own boarding kennel and rescue, so finding space for her was no problem. She was so small and cute compared to my other dogs, and her eyes were kind of buggy, so she became Skeeter Bug. I quickly found her to be my essential companion for a good night's rest, so I decided to adopt her.

I walked into work on Monday with a smile on my face, but after hearing my announcement, my supervisor (at the time) did not support my decision, stating that I already had too many big dogs. Even though my dogs got along with Skeeter Bug just fine, I let her talk me in to interviewing other interested adopters. With her pushing, we found a lady and her daughter that we thought would be a good fit, and my little girl was suddenly taken away.

Before the day was over, I found myself sick with grief because I missed Skeeter Bug so much. The next day, when I called to check on her, the people said that they thought she was sick or grieving because she would not eat. They asked if they could bring her back, but I said no—I'd be right over to pick her up!

My dog was as happy to see me as I was to see her, and since then she has been my best friend for five years and counting. This Chihuahua/pug mix is as cute as a button, and of course, she rules the roost.

 *Stella Koch*

Seeing Her Through

One August day, while helping my in-laws bring food to the local shelter, we noticed a room full of little cages, each with a dog inside. We approached a small pug lying quietly in her cage and were shocked when she did not move. It broke my heart to see such a gorgeous girl so petrified.

We learned that this dog had been dumped for a multitude of reasons. Her original owners were losing their home, and she was the last of the litter. She was partially blind, so no one wanted her. That is, no one but us. We filled out the adoption forms and visited her every day for two weeks while the shelter brought her up to date on her shots and spayed her. We took her for walks, gave her water, provided her with the first doggie bone she had ever chewed, and named her Princess Pia Pia (Pia means "pug" in Chinese).

Our long wait to take our girl home was finally about to end, so we went to the pet store and bought her all the necessary accessories: food bowl, water bowl, crate, bed, shampoo, brush, doggie food, doggie treats, and toys. She was dropped off at our house, and following a quick home investigation, she immediately settled right in on the couch. Princess Pia Pia wasn't potty trained, but after about five days of taking her out to potty every twenty minutes, our efforts paid off.

We started obedience training immediately, and even though she had the standard pug stubbornness, Pia Pia became valedictorian of her beginner class. She also excelled in her intermediate class, but with only two dogs attending, there was no reason to select a "best" (both dogs did well). Her intermediate class trainer saw potential in her to learn more than just basic obedience and suggested we meet with our local therapy dog trainer. Upon meeting our Pug and our family, that trainer encouraged us to train Pia Pia to act as a service dog for my husband who has a terminal illness and needs assistance with hearing and companionship.

Pia Pia passed the initial service dog test with flying colors and went on to become a service dog. With her assistance we believe my husband will live longer. Additionally, her presence has brought our family together in other ways. My stepdaughter no longer hides in her room because she loves to play with Pia Pia. We all go for walks together, and we actually have picnics together instead of eating out so that we can include our pug.

After realizing all Pia Pia was doing for us, we wanted to do what we could for her. We took her to a new vet to make sure all her shots were up to date and see what we could do to save her eyesight. Well, she did need a few shots, and the vet referred us to a specialist about her eyes. The specialist was far away and not cheap, but having her eyes fixed was worth all the travel and expense.

Pia Pia gives us so much love and appreciation. We all know and agree that she made us a closer, better family just by coming into our lives. Our little angel, our pug princess, has been everything we needed plus so much more.

 *Dawn Taylor*

Ace of Hearts

Two weeks before meeting Ace, we lost one of our pugs, Betsy, after she was hit by a car. This loss was so unexpected, and I remember feeling frozen in the moment upon hearing she was gone. Gus, our other pug, also grieved for his sister, best friend, and snuggle buddy. People would tell my husband, Bryan, and me that in time it would get easier. We knew this to be true, but that didn't lessen the hurt. Losing Betsy shattered our house and our hearts, and none of us were doing a very good job of picking up the pieces.

I reached out to Pug Partners rescue for support and to let them know that we would be interested in fostering a pug. We love these animals and believe they all deserve wonderful homes, but we just didn't know if we were ready to take on a new, permanent dog just yet.

After being approved as foster parents, we were immediately asked to foster a six-year-old, fawn, male pug named Ace, who had been a stud at a puppy mill for the majority of his life. This pup was in pretty good shape aside from a few extra pounds and poor dental health. He shook in my arms when I first picked him up, but after five minutes in the car he calmed down. As he laid down his head and looked up at me, I told him, "Welcome to love."

When we got home, Gus gave me an almost angry look as if he was thinking, "Who do you think you are, trying to replace Betsy?" The two dogs didn't fight, but they didn't interact much either, which made me even sadder. Considering how I would feel if someone took my best friend away from me, I could definitely imagine Gus to be hurting and angry, and I wondered whether Gus could ever love another pug.

Compared to Gus, Ace was very round, wrinkly and easygoing. As weeks went by, Ace came into his own, giving me kisses, responding to his name, letting us pick him up, and even pushing past Gus to get all the attention. It made me so happy to see this incredible pug start to enjoy life and understand that he was safe. There is no better compliment.

Ace's presence did not change the fact that the three of us were still hurting from losing Betsy. I told Pug Partners that I loved fostering him, but I didn't know that we were his forever family. After about a month, someone finally applied for Ace. At first I was a little anxious, but then I decided to leave it up to God. Within three days the person had changed her mind, and Ace was still with us.

Ace continued to amaze us as he transformed into a "whole" dog. For us it was hard to image a six-year-old dog who had never seen a treat or a toy, but that was Ace. I'll never forget the first day Ace found our basket of toys. We had always left a few toys out for him, but on this day he found the source of the fun. From then on, we never could keep the toys in that basket for more than five minutes without Ace pulling them all out again.

The New Year approached, and the three of us were finally starting to show signs of life. We were smiling and laughing again, but our hearts still were not ready. During our New Year's Eve party, our guests got to meet the legendary Ace. He was instantly the star of the show, dazzling our guests with his wonderful personality. By midnight everyone was assuring us we were all perfect together. I remember thinking, "How do they know? Why don't I?"

Ace continued to constantly keep us laughing, and Gus even started to come around. They played chase and tug-of-war, and one night we caught them snuggling together—a sight that melted my heart.

About six weeks into fostering Ace, I had to go out of town on business. Bryan sent me a constant stream of text messages telling me all the new, hilarious stuff Ace was doing. Then one night, as I was getting ready for bed and contemplating Betsy's loss and Ace's future, my phone rang with a new text message. It was a picture of Bryan, Gus, and Ace snuggling together in the recliner. The first thought that popped into my head was, "Those are my three boys," and after that moment I never again had to contemplate Ace's future family—he was already home.

I never thought we would survive the hurt of losing Betsy, but our Ace came in and picked up the broken pieces, mending us back together. I wonder sometimes how a dog, broken and battered himself, brought love and happiness and fun back into our lives. But that is when I realized there is only one answer: Ace was the winning card in God's hand—the Ace of Hearts.

 *Jessica Rowe*

A Rescue to the Rescue

Devastated by the unexpected death of our six-year-old pug, Pugsley (a.k.a Puggy), my 1½-year-old pug, Cozmo, who had never been an only pug, was lost and alone. I wasn't ready for another pug and my husband, who adored Puggy, definitely wasn't either. How could I get a new pug so soon after losing Puggy?

But I knew Cozmo was grieving, too, so I made the decision to do it for him. I adopted Izzy from Pug Rescue of New England, and I say "I" because my husband really wanted nothing to do with her. His pug was gone, and to him that was it. He loved Cozmo, but there was never going to be another pug that he would have that special bond with.

I was told Izzy was about four months old. She was fawn but had black coloring down her back and on the back of her legs. When I arrived at the foster home, out from behind a chair came this little, scrawny-looking pug. She had a scar on her eye, which made her rather bulging eyes look even more pronounced. She definitely looked nothing like Puggy! I picked her up and held her in my lap, still trying to decide if I was making the right decision. When she looked up at me and licked my face, I knew this frail pug with the buggy eyes was coming home with me.

When I arrived home, my husband came out to greet me. I'll never forget his first words: "What is that?"

For about two months after adopting Izzy, I slept on the couch with Izzy and Cozmo. Coz was in his usual place by my feet, and Izzy would lie on my chest across my heart. She was so tiny, and those eyes! Sometimes she'd stare at me, and I'd swear her eyes were looking in opposite directions. My husband would often joke, "Who is she looking at? Me or you?" The surgery she had on her eyelids and the tiny purple stitches around her eyes didn't add much to her appearance.

This somewhat homely but sweet, little pug we took in had a tough task ahead: she needed to help us cope with Puggy's death. I don't remember at what point she changed us. Maybe it was how she evolved from this innocent, tiny puppy into the dominant and bossy female that I was warned she would become. She was a handful and I believe her whole "poor me" act was all a scam. She pretended to be innocent and frail. She wanted us to feel bad for her because she was bug-eyed and really not all that cute. But she became pushy, picking on Cozmo by taking all his toys, chasing him around the living room, and biting at the back of his legs, behind, and tail. Outside she would wait for him in this stance that reminded me of a lion waiting to pounce on some poor, unsuspecting gazelle while he did his duties. There would be a stare down, but Cozmo knew it was coming, and Izzy wasn't quite fast enough for his agile maneuvers (I believe his agility training gave him the advantage).

The truth is, she brought us laughter, and Cozmo was not innocent himself. He would instigate the tug of war games or bring his Nylabone over to her and wave it in her face until she tried to go for it, and he would then growl at her. It was his attempt to be dominant, but it rarely worked.

Besides taunting Cozmo, Izzy developed this annoying habit of leaping in the air from the kitchen floor (almost reaching the countertops) over and over again while her food was being put in her bowl. She will not sit quietly like Cozmo. She jumps on your lap anytime you sit down, she jumps on visitors that come to the house, she doesn't listen, she is jealous if Cozmo gets attention, she eats poop, she picks fights with her black lab "cousin," Elle, she takes the toilet paper and runs down the hall with it, she barks and jumps at dogs that are on the TV, even cartoons, and she has even gone so far as taking a piece of food right out of my husband's hand as he was putting it in his mouth! It was his fault, though, because he lets her sit right next to him on the couch when he is eating.

Granted the training issues are mainly our fault; she is spoiled. But it's those eyes! My husband says it's hard to discipline her when she looks at him with that face. Isn't she just the cutest? She sits on the couch beside my husband at night with her head resting on his leg. When she looks up at him, I know he melts. He now refers to her as his dog, and in his eyes she can do no wrong. She is Daddy's little girl, and I think she knew it would turn out this way.

I never thought Cosmo, my husband, or I would survive the early and unexpected death of Puggy. There will always be a hole in our hearts for him, but Izzy has wrapped her little paws around our hearts and holds them tightly.

 *Amy Palmeri*

Four to Adore

As far as pug lovers go, we are at the top of the list. We're right up there with Valentino, the clothing designer who is followed around by a "herd" of at least five or six pugs and Mike Nelson, the Channel Seven weatherman who has a few. Then there's us.

We have four pugs now, two of which my husband, Bob, and I adopted from Colorado Pug Rescue. Hank and Frank are littermates, but they lived in separate homes for a while. One owner died and the other had too many dogs, which is how the pair ended up in rescue together again. We don't know which dog came from which situation, but we speculate sometimes, thinking things like, "This dog is needy. He seems to require a lot more attention than the other," but really we'll never know for sure. When we first met them, it was obvious they were happy to be together again, and they got along with our resident females, Star and Oreo, famously. After the visit, Hank and Frank couldn't wait to come back and move in.

We've since enjoyed each of our pugs' distinctive personalities. Frank is the most verbal: barking, yipping, and jumping up and down on all fours while flapping his paws to greet us when we come home. Star brings a toy in her mouth, trying to look the cute and wanting to play, but Hank is truly the cutest. He doesn't have to do anything to get us to automatically reach down and pet him. Oreo, aptly named for her black coat with a white spot on her chest (her middle name is "Double Stuf" because she is so energetic), is the youngest, and she's always bugging the others. She must think she's the cutest, and of course, she vies for our attention too. Needless to say, coming home is always a joyful occasion.

Frank follows me everywhere and thinks he's my dog. Hank, on the other hand, is Bob's dog, waiting eagerly for Bob to come home from work each day. None of them is perfect, but who is, after all? Frank likes to lick. Star likes to bark a little too much, so she is the designated watch dog. Oreo, the smallest, is also the most aggressive. None of our dogs realize their size, a common trait among pugs. Maybe that's why they are called pugnacious, which describes Oreo perfectly. Hank was a trash dog until we put the trash under the cupboard with a baby lock in place.

Our favorite tease is to ask our dogs, "Did your mother wean you too soon?" They are indeed a bunch of unique little clowns, but they get along. They love it here. We love them. It's a dog's life!

 *Mary Stone*

Doggie Soulmate

At five years old Blaze was surrendered to the pound by his owners, and I still can't figure out why. The shelter workers said they had never seen such a terrified dog when he came in, so they called Compassionate Pug Rescue, and we sprang him *immediately*. My husband and I were to foster him, so a local volunteer pulled him from the shelter while we made the 90-minute drive to go get him.

Blaze turned out to be a joy. Granted, he had unsightly, black skin and crusty lumps on his body, which we feared were tumors but turned out to just be the result of a bad yeast infection. Could this have been why he was surrendered? For the next few weeks we gave him medicated baths and medicine, and he assimilated into our lives as though he had always belonged.

Once he regained his health, we began taking him on home visits to potential adopters, but he constantly hid and cowered—especially from men. Because of this, his chances of finding a new family seemed slim. We already had four pugs, a black lab, three cats, a bird, and a turtle, so although he got along great with us, adopting him as a permanent family member didn't really seem like an option. Regardless, when I came home from work, Blaze ran to greet me as if I had just returned from a long trip. And when I called him, he stopped whatever he was doing to come and sit with me.

The volunteer who picked him up from the shelter had given him a grape box and a blanket as a bed. He slept in the box next to my bed at night until one day we decided to upgrade him. We bought him a real bed, but he wanted nothing to do with it—Blaze just wanted his box. He cried if he couldn't find it and jumped in it if I tried to pick it up. No matter what kind of bed we bought him, Blaze whined for his box. Finally, my husband made a wood frame for the grape box, and we added a pillow with a nice cover in addition to his blanket. Problem solved.

With the box issues out of the way, we still found ourselves at a loss to solve the real problem of finding Blaze a home. It was the holiday season, and the applications for Blaze had stopped coming in. Christmas morning we opened our gifts—the critters, my husband, our son, and me. My last gift was a shirt box, and as I opened it, I saw a homemade story inside. My husband had taken pictures of Blaze doing all the things I love to do, and each picture said how Blaze could help me do them. The last picture was Blaze sitting under our Christmas tree saying that we were each other's gift. My husband had adopted Blaze. He said it was obvious that Blaze was my doggie soulmate.

That was three years ago, and I still cannot think of one reason why someone would surrender him. I am so glad the shelter called Compassionate Pug Rescue to get Blaze because I believe we were meant to be Blaze's forever family.

I am truly thankful and blessed to have such a wonderful family—flesh and furry!

 *Tracey Carr*

A "Snort" Break

No More Bones Peeking Out: Peek-A-Boo, one of over 120 dogs rescued from a puppy mill where the humans just stopped feeding them, was one of the lucky dogs who could be saved. She was a puppy with no coat on the front half of her body—nothing but a hairless rack of bones. We adopted her after she had been returned to the rescue three times for various reasons. She should have been a cowering, shaking, little creature, but she instead chose to let her love abound because she is just so happy just to be alive. Although her growth was stunted from starvation, her coat has grown back, and she's much healthier now that we've provided her with nutritious food that addresses her allergies. She'll always have feet and ears that are too big for her body and a head that is too small, but her loving, happy, playful nature makes her just perfect to us. *-Susan Friis*

Olympugans: How many times can two male pugs take turns peeing on one blade of grass sticking up through the crack in the driveway? If you ask "Pee" and "Repee" (real names Mugsy and Bud), they'll tell you, "To infinity and beyond!" They take their outside duties so seriously that we're lobbying for a new pug Olympic sport in their honor: synchronized peeing! *-Beth Herrick*

Foster to Founder

Lily is the pug who started it all here in Omaha. Someone found her wandering the streets of O'Neil, Nebraska and turned her in to the local shelter. The shelter workers believed she was from a puppy mill because of how skinny she was and the fact that she was still in the process of "drying up" after having had a litter. The shelter then called Midwest Pug Rescue (MPR), who contacted me, since I had adopted from them once before, to ask if I could find her a foster home nearby. My husband, Matt, and I decided to give fostering a try, since we were in the process of finding our dog, Rocky, a new sister.

When Lily arrived in our home, everything was new to her: stairs, the television, dog treats, grass, cement, doors, and walls. But of course, her favorite new experience was home-cooked meals. She would walk around the whole house just smelling the air. After about a month, she started to settle in, getting into our routine and acting like a normal, cuddly pug.

Lily is not fond of men, but she has grown attached to me. She follows me everywhere and never leaves my side unless we are at Grandma's. She's still hesitant with strangers, even women, but she is gradually coming around.

I cannot express how grateful I am to Lisa with MPR for allowing me to foster Lily and fall in love with her. It was because of Lily that we started Pug Partners of Nebraska, a rescue based out of Omaha. Watching Lily bloom into the wonderful dog she is has been a great experience, and I love helping other fosters and adopters to have similar experiences with rescued dogs. Lily, along with the other dogs we've placed in new homes because of her, is truly living the life she deserves today.

 *Jessica Kamish*

Moe on the Go

Moe is proud to be from Michigan. Detroit, Michigan to be exact, which is otherwise known as "Moe-town." He was planning to spend all his days enjoying the Rock City, but his owners launched him into an adventure he could never have imagined when they left him with Michigan Pug Rescue (MPR).

After a few months with his foster family and pug foster brother, Chang, Moe was ready to be adopted. This is when my husband and I come into the picture, a couple of Northwestern grad students ecstatically awaiting the arrival of the first dog either of us has ever owned. After months of planning and making sure we were ready for the responsibility, we found Moe online and immediately knew he was ours. Luckily MPR also agreed that we would be the right home for Moe. As soon as we heard the news, we jumped in the car and excitedly drove the 300 miles from Chicago to Detroit, having no idea how much our lives were about to change!

We walked in the door of the MPR founder's home and entered a room packed with happy, playful pugs. We wondered to ourselves, "Which one will be joining our family?" The founder said, "Here's Moe," and just like that, Moe became a part of our lives forever. Being first time "parents," we were definitely a little nervous about how we would stack up. It certainly didn't help our jitters when Moe's foster parents informed us that he wasn't the best passenger in cars. Poor little Moe cried all the way to Chicago, but after five long hours, he had successfully made the move to the Land of Lincoln.

It took a little time for Moe to teach us how to properly care for him. As his note from his foster mom said, "I like to be good, but sometimes I don't listen to you. Just be patient—I do listen eventually!" Indeed, patience was the key, as the first week Moe didn't listen too well at all. We didn't have a backyard and would spend hours getting Moe to go potty on the leash. After multiple days of two-hour potty sessions (in the middle of finals week, no less), I was in tears thinking we might have to return Moe. But MPR was looking out for us because as soon as we returned home, our rescue outreach volunteer gave me a call. She knew exactly what to say to assure me that Moe would be able to adjust and become a part of our family. It was just going to take some time.

Our routines and Moe's routines eventually did get in sync, and Moe became a fast favorite of our friends, Lindy and Duane. They were planning to get a dog and had been considering a pug as an option. Moe must have sensed an opportunity because as soon as they came over, Moe climbed up on the couch behind Duane and strategically rested his chin right on Duane's shoulder. Needless to say, Moe sealed the deal that night for them to get a pug—specifically a cutey-pie named Hamilton from MPR. We had to hand it to Moe for securing himself a pug friend and playmate, which makes us wonder if our pug is smarter than we think.

We all lived happily in our apartment until graduation. Moe even grew to love car rides, especially because they normally involved a visit to Hamilton's house. Then Moe bid farewell to the beaches of Lake Michigan and made the move with us to Seattle.

Now we're in Seattle for good, and Moe seems happy to be settled here in the Emerald City. He is not a fan of the rain, but he likes a lot of other things about living here: the eco-friendliness (he is a "recycled dog" after all), the great hiking (but no hills, please), the dog-friendly companies, and the dog friendly bars (just water, thanks!). Above everything else, Moe's favorite thing in the world is meeting new people, so it doesn't really matter where he lives. He can hang with anyone, be it felines, canines, or humans, and he even enjoys going to the vet. It doesn't make a difference if they poke and prod him, he just loves the socializing.

Though we may have left Detroit, our hearts will always reside in Moe-town.

 *Erin Metzger*

A Bittersweet Tail

Miles, my black pug, was the world to me. He was my sidekick from puppy to five years of age, accompanying me to work, riding in the car, going for walks, making me laugh, and listening as I cried to him about any horrible days. He always seemed to understand me and shared his love with my family too. In June of last year, we vacationed in Florida and had a few fun-filled days of sun and kayaking. But then tragedy struck, and Miles unexpectedly passed in his sleep.

I was a wreck and didn't think I would recover, despite having the support of my husband of 26 years and our three wonderful daughters. While in Florida, I had to find a place to have my best friend cremated, and then I had to carry him home. I was consumed by feelings of guilt, wondering if I shouldn't have taken him on our trip. My family thought another pug might help to take away some of the hurt, but that idea felt wrong to me. Miles had just died, and I questioned whether I was a bad pug mom for even entertaining the idea of seeking a new companion so soon. Amidst my struggle with this decision, I peeked at some pug websites just to test the water. What I found was an adoption site, a concept that was completely new to me.

I have residency in both Pennsylvania and Florida, but I reside mostly in Pennsylvania. The rescue site was for Central Florida Pug Rescue (CFPR), so I doubted they would adopt to me because of the limited time I spent in the state and my distraught emotional state. Much to my surprise, the rescue agreed to help me. I was amazed at their kindness and understanding of my situation.

Back online at CFPR's adoption page I fell in love with a fawn two-year-old named Jackson's picture and profile. I completed the requisite paperwork, and a volunteer came to my house for a pre-adoption inspection. Soon thereafter I met Jackson. I was still reeling from the loss of Miles and felt I was betraying him by loving Jackson, but I couldn't deny that Jackson would be a great addition to my life.

I adopted Jackson and immediately quickly found out that this sweet dog only wanted love and more love. During the car trip from Florida to Pennsylvania, Jackson rode like a champ. His arrival in Pennsylvania was the first time the rest of his adoptive family met him, and they all took to each other immediately. Jackson was thrilled to have more hands to scratch him, pet him, and throw around his toys.

This smart pug learned his schedule quickly. He gets up for work on Monday through Friday. He knows he has to eat and potty before we leave for the office. Once Jackson is at work, he says hello to all the employees and then lies on his bed in front of a huge window facing a road. He watches traffic and barks when someone walks by his window, and although occasionally he barks at customers, he's not too bad. He snacks during the day and sometimes goes across the street to the pet store for a treat. The store clerks make a fuss over him, and he puffs out his chest as if to say, "I'm the man!"

After work Jackson takes snuggle time *very* seriously. Around 9:00pm Jackson crawls on someone's lap and expects that person to snuggle him until bedtime. He doesn't accept any excuse for a change in this schedule he has adopted.

As a Florida native, Jackson had never seen snow before living with us. To my surprise, he loves it! He runs around in circles and plows through some serious snow accumulations. When taking a break from all the fun, he proudly looks up at me with a white, snow-covered muzzle. His bravery with snowstorms is a reflection of how he's handled his entire transition into our lives. I am confident that the love we give him makes him feel secure in knowing he will not be uprooted again.

Jackson has been with me for over eight months now, and it seems like he has always been mine. I still have teary eyes when I think of my Miles and see his pictures, but I guess I always will. Jackson rescued me from sadness and depression, teaching me an important life lesson: Finding a new love does not require me to forget about the love I received from my previous companion. They can both reside together within my heart.

 *Trish Kerver*

Fank, Who?

One night I received a call asking if I would be willing to foster a dog named "Fank" with a skin condition. Since I have a dog of my own, of course my first question was "What kind of skin condition?" My second question was "What the heck kind of name is Fank?"

I was told that a pug/Boston terrier mix was dropped at a shelter along with his five puppies and their momma. The reason they were relinquished was that the female started losing hair and itching during her pregnancy. Since giving birth, the hair loss and itching spread to the male and the puppies. Of course, when I first heard what had happened to these little guys I was irate. I mean, how could someone just dump their dogs because they were itchy?

Upon further consideration, I was still angry that these people had bred their dogs at all, but after getting past that, I conceded that having seven dogs with hair falling out could have been pretty scary. It made me feel thankful to rescue groups for spending the time and money to help dogs in these kinds of situations.

Colorado Pug Rescue agreed to take the female and the puppies, and I was to foster the male on behalf of MidAmerica Boston Terrier Rescue. Because I didn't want to keep him sitting in a cage longer than necessary, I decided not to wait for a transport volunteer and to instead take the hour-long drive to the shelter and get him myself.

Boy, was I glad I did. The shelter had performed skin scrapes and found nothing, so they decided not to treat him at all. This poor little guy was so itchy when I arrived that I was surprised he wasn't bleeding from clawing himself. It turned out that they also hadn't given his records much of a look, or they would have noticed that his name was "Frank," not "Fank." Someone had just inputted it into the computer wrong (mystery solved!).

Back home Frank and I went right to the vet to get to the bottom of things. The vet surmised that it looked like *Cheyletiella*, a mite issue that could be easily treated with Frontline. Because we didn't know for sure what was going on, we decided to go with a few other interventions as well. Our guess was that the family who had relinquished Frank had assumed the dogs had mange and started dipping all of the dogs in a mange bath, which led to further skin irritation. It seemed obvious as well that his living conditions were pretty nasty because the worst of it was on his bottom and underside.

Frank was very uncomfortable for the first couple of nights, and none of us got much sleep. He wasn't neutered either, and it seemed like every dog he met was put off by him. Frank was never aggressive, although he was somewhat of a humper, but other dogs just didn't really like him. Although it would certainly have been my preference, he couldn't be neutered right away because of his skin.

This is the point in the story where I tell you what saints my parents are. They are always willing to take our dog(s) when we are traveling, and this time Frank's arrival coincided with a weekend trip to the West Coast. Like good parents they volunteered to take Frank along with our adopted Boston Terrier, but they had no idea what they were in for. Let's just say that one of email updates I received from them started with, "Frank just peed on your mother's pillow..." Did I chuckle? Sorry, mom, I did.

Upon my return I talked with our rescue group about Frank's marking issue, and they suggested a belly band. What a lifesaver (or couchsaver, rather)! Essentially it's just a pee-proof band that wraps around the "male contours" and sticks to itself on his back with Velcro. A feminine or incontinence pad is inserted, and then when he pees, he does it on himself instead of the furniture. Sure, I had to wipe Frank off and change the pad, but the idea is that they eventually get the picture. Additionally, I had to remember to take it off when I put him outside to legitimately do his business. The rescue group sent me a band, but before I received it, I just wrapped Frank in a dish towel, and he looked like he was wearing a toga.

After about a month, Frank's skin cleared up, so he could be neutered and put up for adoption. He found a great mom who was able to take him to work with her, which was perfect because he had been going to my office with me and *loved* interacting with people. As it goes every time, I was sad to see him leave, but I'm confident he's in a clean, loving home. If anyone deserved it, he did.

 *Kyla Duffy*

Sarge in Charge

Found as a stray, Sarge was placed in a foster home in Kansas with 15 other pugs. Pandemonium reigned when I met him; pugs were barking, jumping, and all 14, aside from Sarge, were clamoring for my attention. And then there was Sarge, trotting around the corner in his quiet confident way. How could he have been available for adoption for several months with no bites? This big, gorgeous, male pug, with a deformed jaw and a funny tongue that never quite stayed in his mouth, was coming home with me!

Experts say that rescued dogs usually have a transition period of at least a few days or weeks in a new home while they get to know you, but Sarge and I only needed a few moments. It was the first look, the first touch, the first words: "Hey, big guy! Ever heard of Minnesota?" He slept in my arms that first night while we were squeezed together in my daughter's tiny, college apartment. And the next day driving north I was so excited. "He's probably only five or so," I told myself, "I'll have him a really long time!"

Sarge was excited, too, and he quickly became the leader of my pack. He had all the right traits: loyal, loving, intelligent, intuitive, kind and gentle, friendly, and never overbearing. We quickly found that Sarge's foster mom had chosen the perfect name—he was definitely our little sergeant.

Our home has a forever changing "pug posse," as we adopt seniors and special needs pugs. Assertive but never aggressive, Sarge would let the new pugs know with a gentle nudge that he was in charge. "Okay!" my new pug, Boomie, easily told him. "You da man!" They became fast friends though they were quite the odd couple with Sarge being big and calm and Boomie being small and crazy. They struck the perfect balance, and what fun they had! Their favorite pastime was sitting on the couch, soaking up the sun, and catching some zzzz's while waiting for mom.

Sarge became my best friend and went everywhere with me. He was the poster pug for how to behave in the car: sit up straight, don't wiggle out of your harness, no unnecessary barking! With his open and adventurous spirit, he was game for anything I threw his way. He became quite a hit at the nursing home where he regularly visited my mom with my dad and me. When we walked through the doors, the call would go out: "Sarge is here!" He would sit patiently next to whoever wanted to pet him for as long as they needed. Mom no longer talked, didn't recognize us, and rarely smiled, but oh, how she smiled when Sarge arrived! His presence made the visits so much easier. Dad and I would look at each other with tears in our eyes.

My beloved father passed away one winter day, and exactly one year later mom died, too, both on my birthday. In less than 18 months, I lost my parents, my wonderful father-in-law, Mugsy the pug, and the irreplaceable, little, stray cat who made her home with us for 18 years. The amazing Sarge seemed to know how much I needed him, and he never left my side, serving as my anchor through the very difficult time.

But our time together would be limited. Sarge was diagnosed with prostate cancer a year and a half after coming home. He lived for almost two years after his diagnosis, which amazed his doctors. I would have done anything to save him, but sadly, there were no treatment options. I know in my heart that he stayed for me until he knew he could safely pass me into Boomie's care. "Take good care of Mommy, little one," he said. "She needs us."

We lost Sarge about a year ago but continue to rescue older and unwanted pugs. Two more have made their way home since Sarge left, and another is soon to follow. Sadly, one of the older gents was only able to stay for nine months. I know he is waiting for me along with Sarge and all the others.

Oh Sargie! Our time together was so precious and so short. You were truly one in a million! Your love, devotion, and trust knew no bounds. Even when I held you and said goodbye, you looked at me and wagged your tail. You saw me through the most difficult times in my life. The gifts you gave me are immeasurable.

The lessons you taught me are endless. You are the reason I will always take in "used dogs." Thank you my forever, little, furry friend. You are my angel; you are my Sarge.

 *Beth Herrick*

A Gift from Lilo

Last summer was probably the worst I have ever had as I watched my sweet pug, Lilo, slowly die from cancer. She passed in early August, and the only one who took it harder than me was my other pug, Lorenzo. He wandered around the house howling and crying, so we thought that before the school year began again, we should get Lorenzo a new companion for the long days ahead.

As a tribute to Lilo, we decided we would rescue another female pug who was in desperate need of a loving family. I searched the Internet and found Chloe at a rescue about four hours from our home. I contacted them and was told a breeder surrendered her, and they suspected she had been severely abused. Chloe was extremely timid and needed a new home with people experienced in socializing abused animals. Lilo had been abused by her previous owners, too, but she truly bloomed in her years with us, so I felt we were up for the challenge.

From the minute I laid eyes on Chloe, I knew Lilo had led me to her. She was extremely underweight and very afraid. I could count her ribs, and she had no hair on her neck and chest. For the first couple of weeks after taking her home, we had to crawl into the crate to get her out to go potty and give her pets and love. She would shake all over every time we touched her, but eventually she began approaching me very cautiously for attention during the day when I was the only one home. It helped to have another spoiled pug in residence, as Lorenzo showed Chloe how great all the attention could be, and after about six weeks, Chloe began coming out of her crate to allow my sons and husband pet her, too.

When we had Chloe's teeth cleaned, she needed all her bottom, front teeth and four molars extracted. Twice she's also needed veterinary attention for cysts between her toes, which we understand will be a lifelong issue because of her splayed feet, a common attribute among breeding dogs who have been kept in wire cages their whole lives.

I find it hard to express the joy I feel with every milestone Chloe reaches. She is now a healthy, happy pug who runs and plays in the snow with her brother and yips and barks when it's time for dinner. I am amazed that, after all she has suffered at the hands of humans, she is able to snuggle up to me now and give me kisses. She makes a noise that sounds almost like a purr deep in her chest as she lies next to me getting her ears scratched.

I don't think Chloe's fear will ever truly be gone. She will run and hide when a stranger comes into our home and shake and cry on the way to the vet. But there is one big difference for her now—she will never have to face her fears alone or know the pain and loneliness of her first four years because we will be here for the rest of her life.

I think of Lilo every day and say a prayer to thank her for sending Chloe into our lives.

 *Carrie Ortiz*

A "Snort" Break

Yo, Gilliam! Although we live in Philadelphia, we adopted our pugs from Michigan Pug Rescue. Ironically, someone in Michigan loved the movie Rocky and named the pugs after "Rocky" the fighter and "Micky" the coach/manager. The Rocky films are all based and filmed in Philadelphia where we live, so I thought it only fitting to tour the pug-men around the city when they first arrived. I took photos of them in front of the "Rocky steps" at the Philadelphia Museum of Art where Rocky the Pug-man got a chance to meet Rocky...the statue. -*Gina Gilliam*

Clifford Saves the Night: Tank has the breadth of a bulldog, the height of a pug sandwich (two stacked on top of each other), and the girth of a bull. He had been surrendered to rescue because of his snoring *problem,* for which he had to have surgery. He didn't snore much for the first few nights at home with us because he just couldn't get to sleep. But by the third night, I realized that I had forgotten to unpack the "stuff" that accompanied him, including a "Clifford the Big Red Dog" stuffed toy, which turned out to be Tank's magic sleeping pill. Tank was in heaven, sleeping with his nose nestled into the stuffed toy, which softened the snoring and soothed him. Though he still sleeps with Clifford, he's now willing to snuggle with us, too. -*Bette Luck*

Scootin' Along

I was working at a retail store with a woman who also had a small, pug breeding operation at home. She came to work one day and told me about one of the pug babies that always ended up inside the food bowl. She thought he was just more aggressive than the rest, until she noticed that he was not able to walk on his front paws. He scooted around on his elbows and was unable to stand up to the bowl. Three days later she told me he was getting sores on his elbows and that her husband told her they would have to *get rid of him.*

I told her they could do no such thing. "You bring him to me! I'll take him," I said.

The woman was delighted and brought Scooter to me the next day. His front legs seemed to be locked into a bent position, but his paws worked fine. I splinted his paws so he was forced to use them instead of his elbows. He was walking on his paws, even with bent elbows, in no time. X-rays showed that the bones in his elbows were formed incorrectly, which according to the vet, no amount of physical therapy could help. So I took him home to give him the best life I possibly could.

As time has passed, it has become obvious that Scooter *is* happy and has no clue that he has a problem. Sometimes people give us funny looks when we walk the neighborhood, but we just hold our heads high. Scooter is king of our home, and he goes to visit my aging parents once a week as a therapy dog. My father had a stroke about nine years ago and suffers from left-side paralysis. The two are a pair, and they always nap together.

Scooter is also great with my 20-month-old granddaughter and my six-year-old grandson, who has a little stuffed animal pug named Scooter that he sleeps with every night. "Scooter" travels everywhere with him, and we hope to soon find him a real rescued pug with whom he can share his adventures.

 Connie Conner

Patience Pays Off

We lost our two-year-old pug, Otis, to a car accident on my son's 13th birthday. To try and fill the hole he left in our hearts, we decided to save a dog from the dreaded, local pound. It is a very rare instance that the pound would even see a purebred pug, much less keep one for almost three months with no takers. But there sat Kirby, the five-or-six-year-old, prematurely-graying pug who had just about outstayed his welcome.

Kirby's toenails were grown into his paws, and a permanent ring of missing fur around his neck caught my eye immediately. His fearful demeanor, coupled with his appearance, were signs that this guy had obviously had a tough life. The first thing Kirby did was attack me when I went to pet him, which was a bad sign. Purebred or not, if I couldn't get him to trust me enough to take him home, the shelter would most certainly put him down.

I visited him daily, and on the seventh day of my visits, Kirby actually came to me, not only refraining from biting me but actually putting his paw on my lap as I bent down to pet him. It was a miracle. Kirby was still skittish and his affection was short-lived, but he was slowly making progress. We took him home and then to the vet to have his toe nails cut out of his pads. From that point on, we needed to have them filed every couple weeks because the quick had grown down too far to ever clip them normally.

Kirby and I spent a lot of time together. We took walks and car rides, and he eventually graduated to sleeping in bed with us. He became the most loyal, loving pet we ever had. When we moved to a new home approximately six months later, Kirby frantically followed me around as I packed to ensure I wasn't leaving him behind. Upon arriving at the new home, Kirby threw himself on my lap and gave me the first and only kiss I ever saw Kirby give anyone. He was just grateful that we wanted him, and he wouldn't be returning to local shelter.

Most people were surprised at how smart and well-behaved Kirby had become. Though he never learned to truly trust anyone but me, our bond became unbreakable. Sadly, two years after adopting him we learned he had *autoimmune anemia,* a dysfunction of the immune system causing antibodies to attack red blood cells. Under veterinary guidance we tried desperately to treat his illness but were eventually forced to accept his fate and lay him to rest to stop his suffering.

Kirby is gone but not forgotten. His memory still lives in our hearts, and I know he awaits me at the Rainbow Bridge.

 *Jennifer Schumacher*

Life Lessons

I never much cared for dogs. Thanks to my mother, I grew up thinking that they were all just unsanitary animals who would infest our home with fleas and bacteria. So when my husband moved me to Florida from upstate New York and I complained about being lonely, his suggestion to get a little dog for company was met with disgust. Then one day we were watching a dog show on TV, and I fell in love with this tiny dog by the name of Cosmo, an Affenpinscher. What the heck was an Affenpinscher? I didn't know, but he was darn cute with his smooched-in face and under bite. I was in love, but little did I know that our quest to find me an Affenpinshcer would lead me to so much more.

Lesson 1: Relaxation

Our search led us through the internet to the sleepy little town of Bunell, Florida, where we pulled into the driveway of an old, small house. The woman brought out this little, black puppy, no bigger than the size of my hands, and my heart melted. We'll take him! So we gave her our $400, and our Affenpinscher, Vern, promptly peed all over me. At home Vern grew and grew. This eight-pound "purebred Affpinscher" grew to 25 pounds!

Vern appeared to be half French bulldog, but the joke's on the breeder because Vern was one of a kind and worth a million. If Vern had thumbs and a voice, he'd be human. He showed me what it was like to experience the true love that a dog can give a human, and after five years we decided he should also have a canine companion to love. But this time I knew better, and I swore that I would never "buy" another dog. I would rescue. Vern taught me that I could help a less fortunate animal....just take a deep breath, give it a try, and relax...

Lesson 2: Compassion

And then there were two! I found my sweet Ramona Rose on Compassionate Pug Rescue's website and named after my Uncle Raymond, who passed away the week Ramona came into our lives. Ramona was a severely abused pug used in a puppy mill for breeding. She was six pounds and hairless with a left eye so damaged that it had to be removed. She had *mastitis* (a breast infection), *mange* (a skin disease caused by parasitic mites), fleas, and *ehrlichiosis* (an infection of the white blood cells caused by bacteria).

My husband asked, "Couldn't you have found a prettier one?" but her picture spoke to me. Though I loved her she proved to be a challenge, marking my home and bed and attacking Vern, which continued for about a year. She tested and dared us not to love her, but lots of carpet cleaner and one mattress later, she's 24 pounds, sheds all over the house, loves her brother, is the biggest cuddle-bug ever, and has given back our affection and patience tenfold. She can't see, and we've subsequently had to have one of her ear canal's removed due to severe scarring, so she doesn't hear very well, but her oversize heart taught me compassion.

Lesson 3: Patience

Being the glutton for punishment that I am, my husband and I thought it would be wonderful if we could help the rescue out by becoming foster parents. Shortly after filling out the paperwork, we got called to foster and drove to Georgia to gather our new charges: two pugs at Jellystone Campground. One's name was Miles. He was microchipped, but the owners changed their phone number, so they obviously didn't want their dog. We didn't know the name of the other one, so we named him Yogi.

Yogi was adopted within two weeks, but Miles, who turned out to be a pug/Shar Pei mix, was the epitome of the word "naughty." He was crazy: jumping, biting, and barking, going out of his way to be bad! My husband said, "If we place him for adoption, we'll probably get him back because he's so naughty. We might as well just keep him."

And just like that there were three. Like with Ramona, it took Miles one full year to calm down and know he was home, but now he's the house comedian, and we don't know how we ever lived without him. He taught me patience.

Lesson 4: Sympathy and Tolerance

The rescue beckoned again, asking if we could foster a 12-year-old, female pug whose owner had passed away. Neurological damage to her back end causes her to drag her feet, and her poop falls out at random.

"Uh, sure!" we said, and Chewie is now part of our household. She's still technically up for adoption, but the rhetorical question remains, "Will anyone adopt an elderly, crippled, incontinent pug?" You be the judge.

Lesson 5: Gratitude

I love them all equally and thank God every day that he brought them to me. Some rescued animals come with issues—boy, did ours come with issues—but the unconditional love and appreciation they give their humans in return cannot be measured. My dogs have seen me through elation, heartbreak, love, and change. They may not be the prettiest dogs, and they may not all be purebred, but they are my rocks, the best, most loving creatures I have even known. I will always rescue, and I will always stand ready to correct those who think of dogs the way my mom did. One day with a dog and it's easy to see why so many families feel incomplete without one.

 *Vicky Sydorowicz*

The Dog with Nine Lives

I can't say that I was overly excited to get him. After all, at the time I had a houseful of my own dogs and other fosters. But Colorado Pug Rescue (CPR) had a growing list of older pugs needing foster homes, so we decided to open our home to Nick and hope for the best.

At the age of 13, Nick was a victim of divorce. Sadly, this was not the first time that he had lost his home—in fact, it was the eighth. He'd spent the last four years outside, 24 hours a day, seven days a week, with human contact limited to the family's children throwing food into the yard for him.

Nick's health had also been neglected. He was obese, had only three teeth, and suffered from horrible arthritis, which was most likely due to a variety of issues: age, inadequate care, and many years spent out in the cold of winter.

Well, there I was, face-to-face with my new charge. I began to feel a mix of excitement and anxiety as I wondered how he would get along with my crew. He was a quiet passenger on the long ride home, and by the time we were halfway there, he was sound asleep. I hoped this was a sign that he was comfortable with me.

In the days that followed, Nick fit in quite well. He had the occasional squabble over food if another dog walked too close to his food dish, but overall it was almost as if he had always been with us. All members of our family had nicknames, and Nick's became Chunk because of his portly stature.

As the days turned into weeks, I became extremely attached to Chunk. Although he followed his dad everywhere, Chunk was, in my mind, *my* boy. I grew to love him, and as time passed I couldn't see our lives without him. Then in August Chunk was diagnosed with cancer, and before his surgery we decided to adopt him and make him a permanent member of our family. Luckily our Chunk is a fighter, and he sailed through his surgery, only losing his three remaining teeth because they were so loose it was better to have them pulled while he was under.

So here we are, proud owners of a 13-year-old, cancer-free, toothless pug, and I couldn't have been more pleased. After being with us for only a few months, Chunk was feeling right at home. His favorite thing had become riding the tractor with his dad with a look of accomplishment, dignity, and satisfaction on his face. I watched them for hours riding up and down the road, which sometimes caused me to laugh hysterically and other times just made me smile. I felt like the luckiest girl in the world.

Six months after his cancer surgery, Chunk became extremely ill. He was lethargic, vomiting, and had a horrible fever. The vet determined it to be *aspiration pneumonia*, a serious inflammation of the lungs. Chunk spent five weekdays at the vet on IV fluids and antibiotics. At night he would come home with us, so he could be monitored 24 hours a day. It was painful for me to see my little boy feeling so horrible, unable to keep food or water down, and barely having the energy to lift his head. But once again our tough little cookie beat what everyone thought he couldn't. Some folks joke that he has nine lives, and I, in my heart, hope he does.

All of my pugs, fosters and forevers, are special to me. The breed is unlike any other I have met. They are happiest with their people, and they never meet someone or something they don't like.

Chunk, too, has that special thing. Maybe he seems *more* special to me because of his rough life, the neglect he suffered, and the many homes he went through. All I know is that I couldn't love my Funky Chunky Monkey any more than I do today. He is one spectacular little dog who is finally getting the love and king-sized bed he always deserved.

 *Kasi Rishel*

Chipper Brings Cheer

When one door closes, another opens. Following the unexpected death of my young Hopper, I was empty and looking for more within myself. My friend, Wendi, mentioned two pugs needing a foster home, and suddenly, I felt this was the calling I'd been searching for. I spoke with my husband about it, and we decided to give fostering a try.

When my husband and I met Wendi at the local dog park to collect our new fosters, she showed up with only one pug; apparently the female had just died. My heart just broke, and I looked sadly at the lone male pug. His name was Chipper, and he was a large-framed, senior guy, who was overweight at 35 pounds. Nevertheless, he was a handsome boy, and I fell in love with his white face.

When we got home, Chipper didn't want to eat, but eventually crumpled liver treats on his kibble did the trick. He spent part of his first night sitting in the middle of the living room, emitting a lonely howl, so I did my best to comfort him. When I scooped him up and gave him lots of love, I was sure that my new purpose was to pass on my love for Hopper to other pugs in need.

After three weeks in our home, I asked my husband if we could adopt 12½-year-old, arthritic Chipper. It took a special heart to adopt this boy, but I knew he had found his forever home with us. In the first five months we had Chipper, he lost 10 pounds and became alert, healthy, and happy.

A few months later he had a seizure, so we rushed him to the emergency vet. X-rays showed an enlarged heart, which is common in senior dogs, and a very narrow, possibly collapsing trachea. The vet said a lack of oxygen could have caused Chipper's seizure, but since that had been the first seizure we'd seen, we decided to monitor him instead of placing him on medication.

Chipper did great. His baby "sister," Phoebe, was his caretaker, always grooming him, cleaning his ears, and sleeping by his side. Chipper's love of food returned quickly after his seizure, with his favorites being watermelon, yogurt, and popsicles. He became extremely attached to me and often got jealous when my other pug, Boley, came near me. Chipper would hobble over to me while I was petting Boley and give him a bump with his chest. It was the cutest thing.

Unfortunately, Chipper had a stroke, causing him to lose the ability to use his arthritic right front leg. The next 24 hours went by fast as we sedated Chipper to help him rest. During his waking periods I worked with him to help him regain mobility. I built a make-shift support and put it under his front legs, which allowed him to walk. Miraculously, between my love for him and his determination, Chipper regained use of his leg within a week. My vet could not believe how he recovered.

From then on out we took each day with Chipper as it came. Less than two months after his stoke, he went blind. He had a hard time adjusting to his blindness and often got frustrated, but he eventually learned his way around the house and bumped his head less. Soon after, he was thrown another curve ball—he lost his hearing. Once again he rallied, and his nose became his communicator. He quickly learned my smell, and when I would come home from work and kneel down to him as he slept, his eyes would open with excitement, he'd gather up enough energy to stand, and then he'd let out a loud, "WOO," to let me know he missed me. At dinner time he had no problem finding his way to the kitchen.

About a year and a half after Chipper's stroke, we gave him our utmost love by setting him free from his worn body. He was 15½ years old, grand and grumpy to the end. In the three wonderful years we had Chipper, we had some challenges, but our love got us through. Chipper taught us much about patience, determination, dedication, and unconditional love, and he helped fill the emptiness I felt after losing Hopper. Loving Chipper, a senior dog, gave me the opportunity to experience some special little miracles.

 *Sharon Hoffman*

Pawdiatric Nurses

My wife and I are both pediatric nurses and parents of a special-needs son. He was fortunate enough to be given a pug puppy from a breeder with whom he was doing some volunteer work, which was all it took to plant the love of all things puggy in our family.

We were watching our local shelter's website for pugs when we finally saw a listing for a small-statured female. She'd been dropped off in the night box and had obviously just been bred. We adopted her straight away and were told we could pick her up in three days. The next day, however, she started coughing, so the shelter asked us to retrieve her immediately. We did, and we were lucky that this poor dog's kennel cough did not infect our other pug, our Dachshund, or our poodle. She was crowned "Daisy" by our daughter because of her flowery collar, and upon arriving home, Daisy quickly put her motherly instincts to work by bossing our first pug around at every opportunity.

Since two pugs couldn't possibly be enough, I started looking at all surrounding shelters for another, and I found a listing for a pug named Buster. His family of five years had apparently dumped him to make room for a cat! I assumed my wife would love having a third pug, so I went and picked him up. On the way home, I called my wife and put him on the phone. Surprisingly, she was less than impressed. Adding to her reluctance was Buster's gift to our family, kennel cough, and this time everyone got sick. Giving five dogs honey so they could sleep was like being at work for us!

Nevertheless, we got through it, and our household now has two parents, three kids, and five dogs. That means there is a one-to-one dog-to-human ratio. It's perfect! Though picking a favorite dog is like picking a favorite kid—it just doesn't feel right to do so—at times I'd swear the rescued dogs have just a bit more love to give. I notice this especially when I come home from an awful day and need some comfort. They seem to say, "Kent, I know how you feel," and I believe they can truly empathize—despite their rough pasts, they always return the favor of a warm couch and full bowl of food with a lick and some love.

 *Kent Stemen*

A "Snort" Break

Things that Make You Go, "Hmmm..." Eight-year-old Bailey's family said they surrendered him because of their child's allergies, but we had to wonder. The poor dog had infections in both ears, and his skin was covered in hairless, black, scabby spots, pus, and blood. He smelled terrible, and as if all that weren't enough, he was partially blind. A good diet and multiple natural remedies helped to improve Bailey's medical issues, and before we knew it, he was ready for adoption. But Bailey had apparently decided he had already been adopted. He would not leave our sides and climbed over his four-foot high exercise pen to sit in my lap at adoption meet-and-greets, signaling to me he was already home. So even though our daughters are now married and on their own, we still have two spoiled little babies—Bailey and his stepsister, Mischief. *-Debbie Fatt*

Pug Pile: I named him Oliver Twist because of the way he dances in a circle on his hind legs for treats, but his nickname is "Houdini" since he can escape any pen I put him in. He was found on the streets, and his two lingering habits are marking and food guarding. However, seeing him sleeping happily on the big, black chair in the living room with his brother and sister pugs makes it all worthwhile. Whether they're sleeping on top of each other or snuggled up next to me, they're the perfect pile of pugs. *-Janet Sandberg*

Best Friends Forever

I am fondly known in the neighborhood as "the pug lady." Whenever I take a walk with these curly-tailed wonders, people have one of two reactions: point and laugh at the pushed-in pug noses or coo and gush. I got my first pug when I was eleven, and I haven't been right since. Pugs aren't just dogs, you know. They are special creatures, and they know it. My heart melts whenever I see one in person or even in a picture.

That's why after my "warrior princess," Xena, passed away a year ago, I was looking for another girl pug. Bart was her constant companion, and having been together their whole lives, Bart was lost without her. Not being an alpha male, he just didn't have direction in his life. His personality changed, becoming clingy and insecure. Xena was the boss, and now that she was gone, Bart was underfoot *all the time.*

I put my application in to Colorado Pug Rescue with very specific requirements: female, good with other dogs (especially clingy, boy ones), good with children, housetrained, three-years-old or younger, and preferably not having been bred before. I was dead set on all my requirements except the last one. I got a call a few days later from a lady who thanked me for my application and said they would keep it on file, but that they rarely had young girl pugs come in. Most of the ones they receive are old, have been kept in a crate and used for breeding, have not been around people (much less children or dogs), and were thus are not housetrained, either.

Nevertheless, I was hopeful. I knew there had to be the perfect one for our family. She was out there somewhere, probably in need of us, too. I said a prayer for her, wherever she was, and to my surprise, it was answered the next day! The call came on a cold late November evening. She had been relinquished by some breeders who said they didn't want her because "she couldn't hold her puppies." She was about three years old, bone thin, frost bitten, not too friendly, very dirty, and stuffed in a cage with a bunch of other scared, dirty dogs.

She was also little, black, and very cute with bright eyes and soft, shiny fur that a simple bath had restored. She was warming up slowly to her foster family, especially the children, and potty training came naturally to her. Could I pick her up in two weeks? It sounded too good to be true!

The day before I was to meet her and bring her home, her foster mom called and said, "Well, she hadn't made a peep in two weeks. We were wondering if she even could, but it seems she's found her voice and has started barking. A lot. Like, most of the time. Do you still want her?"

Barking we can handle. She's trying to say something, and we just have to figure out what it is. We'll develop our own language together.

When I met her in person, I loved her at first woof. Bart came with me and, of course, went around to *other side* to say hello while she was hiding behind her foster mom. Bad idea. She put him right in his place. It was like she was saying, "I used to be that kind of girl, but I'm not anymore. Back off, buddy!"

Bart, I think, fell right in love. "She's bossy, and I love her!"

We named her Gigi. She's very much the girl we wanted: feminine yet tough, verbal but teachable, very smart, and wanting so much to please. She's good with the little ones, and Bart is back to his old, second-in-command, lovebug self.

Gigi did have issues, just as any previously unloved dog does. I hired a trainer who came to the house and showed us how to "talk" to each other. (Trainers train the people in the house, not the dog, by the way.) Gigi wants to have good manners; the barking was the sound of insecurity. She followed me around for three straight months, afraid to let me out of her sight. Gradually she'd lay in her "place," keeping just her eyes on me. Now, more than a year later, she is content, full of affection, energy, adorable personality, and a love for life. She *was* trying to say something: "I'm a good girl. I just need someone to love and care for me so that my *inner pug* can blossom. I'll be your best friend if you'll just give me chance."

The day I knew I'd heard her correctly was the day I discovered Bart and Gigi napping together in Bart's basket with his favorite toy carrot under Gigi's chin. He doesn't let anyone have that carrot.

She was just waiting to be discovered as our best friend forever.

 *Judy Meurer*

The Principles of Pug Ownership

Hi! My name is Minnie, and I want to talk to you about the principles of pug ownership. I know a lot about it because I own two humans, Bernie and Cheryl, and another pug named Zeke. I came to live with them two months ago when they "adopted" me, but I've been around for 10 years.

Adopted? Who are they kidding? I allowed them to bring me to their home, and after a couple of days, I decided I approved of it and would stay. If anything, I adopted them.

When I was a puppy, I owned a good human. But when he died, his cousin took me in. Here was a guy who just didn't get it. He didn't spend any time with me, didn't obey my commands, didn't feed me well, didn't wash me, and didn't take me to the vet when I was sick. When his cousin finally brought me into the shelter, I hadn't had a bath in a year. I was ill and I stunk—disgusting!

At the shelter they fed me and bathed me, and finally people listened to me, at least some of the time. But there were all these other dogs there competing for attention, many of whom were non-pugs I might add. They're only good for making noise, and occasionally I might sniff their butts, but that's as far as it goes, mind you! So I didn't get the attention I so richly deserve.

Then I went to live with a foster mom named Joan. *Finally!* She accepted orders from me quite nicely and got me good vet care. I had to have a couple of surgeries, and Joan nursed me back to health. I had a great time at Joan's—her cats were fun to chase and her pug, Polo, was the subject of my queenly domain. We became good friends, and I really thought I had found heaven.

Then one day these two goofy people, Cheryl and Bernie, showed up with this crazy pug, Zeke. Zeke got into it with Polo, and I just let him have it. I barked his ear off until he backed away. Zeke quietly climbed into Bernie's lap and hoped no one noticed what a chicken he was. Well, I did. What a weenie!

I thought they were just visiting, but the next thing I knew, I was in their car. Joan was crying, Bernie and Cheryl were crying, and I was wondering why this was happening. Zeke was just being goofy. And then the car backed out without Joan! I stood up in the seat and locked eyes with my dear Joan. I never let hers go until we drove out of sight. I couldn't believe she'd let me go. I was so down.

Bernie and Cheryl took me to their home, which is now mine. I agreed to let them live there in exchange for certain considerations. I walked in and said, "Alright. Who's in charge here?" At first they didn't get it, but I whipped them into shape. I get tasty meals, delicious treats, and I lie in the sun naked whenever I want to. I have my own bed in which I allow the humans and Zeke to sleep, but they know who the boss is.

My new house has a great fenced-in backyard with rabbit squatters living under the gazebo, the shed, and the patio. When I see one, I zip out the door barking, but it always gets away. I bark a lot when they're hiding, too, just to let them know that Her Highness is in residence and will brook no insolence.

Zeke is after me to play with him, but I only flirt with him now and then. After all, if you give in right away, they think they own you. He's a lovable big galoot, and I can feel my heart softening—I'm just what he needs. He's already running after the rabbits again, which is something he stopped when his girlfriend, Cindy, got sick. I learned from Zeke that she died a couple of months before I moved in after having a long and happy life with Bernie and Cheryl.

Cindy owned this place before I did. I know this because there are all these disgustingly sweet pictures on the walls of her, Zeke, and Bernie and Cheryl. (I often wonder why humans always want to ruin pictures of pugs by putting themselves in them.) Although Cindy was quite a princess,

I know I'm the queen. Sometimes my humans accidentally call me Cindy, and then they catch themselves. They get this distant look in their eye, and sometimes they cry. This is when I really like them. If they loved Cindy that much, there's got to be love in there for me.

I figure I'll give them time. I know they're falling in love with me, though I hate it when Cheryl insists on picking me up and giving me noisy kisses. Nevertheless, I'll make a small concession and tolerate them.

Okay, it's time for me to go lie on Bernie's pillow. He thinks that's his spot on the bed, but I know differently. See you around—you'll know me as the one leading around the two humans and goofy Zeke. Bye, Bye!

 *Minnie Blehm-Poskus,
translated by humble scribe,*
Bernie Poskus

A Reason to Hope

L ate one night a tiny, black, female pug was found wandering the streets of a small town in Western Massachusetts. She was sick and in heat, but all the animal control officer could do get her minimal veterinary care and put her in a kennel for the standard, 10-day waiting period to see if someone would claim her.

The vet scanned the pug for a microchip and found one, so the officer called the person associated with the microchip number. That person said she had no idea why she was the contact on the microchip registration, and it must be some kind of mistake. But we know better—she is a notorious backyard breeder who still today has a lonely, male pug tied to a tree in her front yard. Sadly we can't help that dog at this time, but we are thankful this woman did not come to claim the little black pug, so we could help her at least.

After the ten-day waiting period was over, Pug Rescue of New England (PRoNE) immediately sprang the distressed dog from her cell and handed her over to me.

When I saw her, I was simply shocked. Her labored breathing frightened me, and she was a daunting sight: black fur now coarse and brown in many places, several large lumps disfiguring her lower abdomen, back legs extended so far out to the sides that she reminded me of a truck with double tires in the rear. She also possessed an oddly crooked jaw.

During the drive home, she cried, and her breathing became even more labored. Convinced she was in dire straits, I called PRoNE management to discuss options. I sincerely thought I might have to put her to sleep to ease her suffering that very night. PRoNE management advised me to use my judgment, and I elected to drive to an emergency clinic where the vet confirmed my fears that the lumps on her abdomen were mammary tumors, most likely cancerous. Only an X-ray could determine whether the cancer had spread to her lungs. I decided to do the X-ray the next day at my regular vet's office in order to conserve funds for the rescue, so the emergency clinic gave the pug an injection to calm her, and we went home.

The next morning brought new promise when my vet discovered that the pug's "tumors" were actually hernias, which were likely the result of ceaseless, irresponsible breeding. In his opinion, the pug's weight of 10.5 pounds should have deterred anyone from breeding her. My vet also diagnosed Grade III *luxating patellas* (where the knee cap does not properly slide in its groove), a jaw that had been broken and had healed incorrectly, an ear infection, and a kidney infection.

An ultrasound showed damage to both her heart and lungs and revealed that the hernias would be difficult to repair because of their size and location. The vet performing the ultrasound advised against surgery because she could die from the anesthesia. Again, I considered putting her to sleep, but I was not convinced she was ready, and I knew I definitely was not.

It wasn't all good news at the vet that day, but at least she didn't have cancer, so my husband and I decided we would make her as comfortable and healthy as possible and deal with the rest of her problems as they came. We gave her the name "Hope" because we were hoping that she would survive long enough to enjoy the care and affection she had clearly never before received.

Hope was essentially un-adoptable at this time due to her multiple illnesses. Several months passed, and Hope's ear and kidney infections cleared up. She added 1½ pounds to her body weight, and her fur started to become blacker and softer. She perked up a bit and started to learn that a hand coming toward her would bring comfort and love instead of pain and suffering. Eventually Hope craved constant contact with my husband and me.

About five months passed without incident before we noticed that the abdominal hernias were growing larger and impacting Hope's life. We decided to consult another vet for a second opinion, who was willing to perform surgery on the hernias but still cautioned us that it was risky. My husband and I felt the risk was worth it because if the hernias continued to grow, as they likely would, Hope would need to be put to sleep anyway.

Then the best thing that could happen did. Hope came through the hernia surgery with flying colors. The vet was even able to spay her, so she would never have to go through a cycle again. We were told that Hope's uterus was the size of a German shepherd's, indicating that she probably had at least 30 litters during her short lifetime, which they estimated to be between 10 and 12 years based on the condition of her organs. Because of her size, most people think Hope is a puppy or young dog, but she is actually a senior citizen.

My husband and I decided to adopt her. She is only the second dog we have adopted in our more than five years working with PRoNE, so you know how special she is. Hope is thriving and in good health for the most part, despite her luxating patellas and arthritis in her hips.

Hope has lived up to her name and represents what rescue is all about: taking tossed away and unwanted animals, healing them, and placing them in homes where they will be cared for and loved as they should have been from the start.

Even when the path seems insurmountable, there is always a reason to hope.

 *Tammy Cooper*

Puggy Problems

Sometimes the Solution Is Simple: Millie, a puppy mill momma, was not only shy and timid when we met her, but she was also emaciated because her mouth didn't seem to close properly to chew. She had been sent to me along with hard, large kibbles, so I tried feeding Millie the home-cooked food I make for my pugs. She wouldn't go near it until she saw BooBoo eating, and then she decided to try. She loved it! After a month of cooking for her, she began to try the dry puppy food. Her facial muscles tripled in size, and eventually she could eat normally. BooBoo also taught her how to play, conquer stairs, and interact with humans, and Millie has really come around. *-LeahAnn Gill*

Green Bean Diet: My eight-year-old pug, Kirby, was extremely overweight when he was relinquished to rescue, so I put him on the "green bean" diet. Kirby ate between ½ and ¾ cup of dog food and a ½ can of green beans per day. The beans would fill him up without adding weight. I would just heat the beans up a little and add them to the top of dry dog food. When he dropped to a healthy weight, I increased the dry dog food a little. Now he gets between ¾ and 1 cup per day of dry dog food and no beans. He's down from 28 pounds to a healthy 17. *-Cassie Reich*

Puggy Problems

Eyes, Who Needs Them? Dee Dee lost her eyes from injuries, but she seems to have a sixth sense that acts as her navigation system. She runs in the yard as though she can see where she is going, and most people can't tell she is blind. Once in a yard with three other dogs, Dee Dee was the first to notice a squirrel perched on the fence. New places can be a bit of a challenge, but in addition to knowing commands like "sit" and "stay," she learned that "careful" means to stop and be cautious. Her disability never keeps her from having fun and she squeals with excitement when a new person pays her attention. -*Cassie Reich*

One Long Day: Two-year-old JoJo was filthy and skinny with terrible diarrhea. His mouth was full of plaque and his teeth in poor condition. His skin was coming off in patches and he had dark reddish markings all over his body. He also had bi-lateral *luxating patellas* (a knee issue affecting the functioning of the knee cap). Armed with antibiotics and a mandate to put some weight on JoJo, his foster parents took him home. Most pugs don't have a problem gaining weight, but JoJo continued to have diarrhea and vomiting. Blood work showed his digestive issues were most likely a side effect of the poor nutrition and his penchant for eating rocks. After gaining some weight and battling both respiratory and groin infections, he was finally ready for surgery. In one long day he was neutered, had the worst of his two luxating patellas fixed, and was given a dental. JoJo came through surgery with flying colors, and after a few painful days he was back to his usual hyper and precocious self. –*Tammy Cooper*

The Ugly Bugsy

Looking at Petfinder,
What do I see?
An ugly little dog,
Smiling back at me.

"I have to have him!"
I squealed with delight.
His ugly little mug,
Is such a silly sight.

Wandering the streets,
With puppies in tow,
Cold and hungry,
No place to go.

Along came a rescue,
Who swept them away,
Looking for a home where,
Forever he would stay.

Missing some teeth,
Has only one eye,
Other than that,
He's a sweet little guy.

So we went to see,
The dog with the mug.
He just had to be,
My new cuddle bug!

A Pug with a tux?
A dog with a plan.
I knew in an instant,
He'd be my new man.

I took my dog Booger,
Along for the meet.
They sniffed in agreement,
My family's complete.

He's no longer homeless,
Or neglected, you see.
My ugly boy Bugsy,
Is beautiful to me!

 Brandy D. Hacker

About Happy Tails Books™

Happy Tails Books™ was created to help support animal rescue efforts by showcasing the love, happiness, and joy adopted dogs have to offer. With the help of animal rescue groups, stories are submitted by people who have adopted dogs, and then Happy Tails Books™ compiles them into breed-specific books. These books serve not only to entertain, but also to educate readers about dog adoption and the characteristics of each specific type of dog. Happy Tails Books™ donates a significant portion of proceeds back to the rescue groups who help gather stories for the books.

 Happy Tails Books™

To submit a story or learn about other books Happy Tails Books™ publishes, please visit our website at http://happytailsbooks.com.

We're Writing Books About Your Favorite Dogs!

Schnauzer Chihuahua Golden Retriever PUG
DACHSHUND German Shepherd Collie Boxer
Labrador Retriever Husky Beagle ALL AMERICAN
Border Collie Pit Bull Terrier Shih Tzu Miniature Pinscher
Chow Chow Australian Shepherd Rottweiler Greyhound
Boston Terrier Jack Russell Poodle Cocker Spaniel
GREAT DANE Doberman Pinscher Yorkie SHEEPDOG
ST. BERNARD Pointer Blue Heeler

Find Them at Happytailsbooks.com!

Make your dog famous!

Do you have a great story about your adopted dog? We are looking for stories, poems, and even your dog's favorite recipes to include on our website and in upcoming books! Please visit the website below for story guidelines and submission instructions. **http://happytailsbooks.com/submit.htm**